Autism Spectrum Disorder

About the Authors

Dr. Lisa Joseph is a child clinical psychologist. She completed postdoctoral fellowships at Brown University and at the Pediatrics and Developmental Neuroscience Branch of the National Institute of Mental Health Intramural Resarch Program in Bethesda, MD, working with children with autism spectrum disorder (ASD) and other developmental disabilities. Her research interests include repetitive behaviors in children with ASD and differential diagnosis in ASD.

Dr. Latha Soorya is a clinical psychologist and assistant professor of psychiatry at the Autism Assessment Research Treatment and Services (AARTS) Center at Rush University Medical Center (RUMC), Chicago, IL. Dr. Soorya is a clinician–researcher with dual expertise in the evaluation of and evidence-based behavioral interventions for individuals with ASD. Her research interests are focused on improving the efficacy and delivery of outpatient treatments for individuals with ASD across the lifespan. Active research studies include treatment studies targeting socialization and neurocognitive deficits in children with ASD.

Dr. Audrey Thurm is a child clinical psychologist and staff scientist in the Pediatrics and Developmental Neuroscience Branch of the National Institute of Mental Health Intramural Research Program in Bethesda, MD. Her research focus is ASD, and she is especially interested in early diagnosis. Active research studies include natural history studies of autism and related genetic disorders, as well as studies of infants at risk for developing ASD.

Advances in Psychotherapy – Evidence-Based Practice

Series Editor
Danny Wedding, PhD, MPH, School of Medicine, American University of Antigua, St. Georges, Antigua

Associate Editors
Larry Beutler, PhD, Professor, Palo Alto University / Pacific Graduate School of Psychology, Palo Alto, CA
Kenneth E. Freedland, PhD, Professor of Psychiatry and Psychology, Washington University School of Medicine, St. Louis, MO
Linda C. Sobell, PhD, ABPP, Professor, Center for Psychological Studies, Nova Southeastern University, Ft. Lauderdale, FL
David A. Wolfe, PhD, RBC Chair in Children's Mental Health, Centre for Addiction and Mental Health, University of Toronto, ON

The basic objective of this series is to provide therapists with practical, evidence-based treatment guidance for the most common disorders seen in clinical practice – and to do so in a reader-friendly manner. Each book in the series is both a compact "how-to" reference on a particular disorder for use by professional clinicians in their daily work, as well as an ideal educational resource for students and for practice-oriented continuing education.

The most important feature of the books is that they are practical and easy to use: All are structured similarly and all provide a compact and easy-to-follow guide to all aspects that are relevant in real-life practice. Tables, boxed clinical "pearls," marginal notes, and summary boxes assist orientation, while checklists provide tools for use in daily practice.

Autism Spectrum Disorder

Lisa Joseph
Pediatrics and Developmental Neuroscience Branch, Intramural Research Program, National Institute of Mental Health, Bethesda, Maryland

Latha Soorya
Department of Psychiatry, Rush University Medical Center, Chicago, Illinois

Audrey Thurm
Pediatrics and Developmental Neuroscience Branch, Intramural Research Program, National Institute of Mental Health, Bethesda, Maryland

HOGREFE

Library of Congress Cataloging in Publication
is available via the Library of Congress Marc Database under the
Library of Congress Control Number 2014945023

Library and Archives Canada Cataloguing in Publication

Joseph, Lisa, author
    Autism spectrum disorder / Lisa Joseph, Alliant International University, Hong Kong, China, Latha Soorya, Autism Assessment Research Treatment and Services (AARTS) Center at Rush University Medical Center (RUMC), Chicago, Illinois, Audrey Thurm, Pediatrics and Developmental Neuroscience (PDN), National Institute of Mental Health (NIMH), Bethesda, Maryland.

(Advances in psychotherapy--evidence based practice series ; volume 29)
Includes bibliographical references.
Issued in print and electronic formats.
ISBN 978-0-88937-404-1 (pbk.).--ISBN 978-1-61676-404-3 (pdf).--
ISBN 978-1-61334-404-0 (html)

    1. Autism spectrum disorders--Diagnosis. 2. Autism spectrum disorders--Treatment. I. Soorya, Latha, author II. Thurm, Audrey, author III. Title.
IV. Series: Advances in psychotherapy--evidence-based practice ; v. 29

RC553.A88J675 2014   616.85'882   C2014-904947-1
                                                C2014-904948-X

© 2015 by Hogrefe Publishing
http://www.hogrefe.com

PUBLISHING OFFICES
USA: Hogrefe Publishing Corporation, 38 Chauncy Street, Suite 1002, Boston, MA 02111
                Phone (866) 823-4726, Fax (617) 354-6875; E-mail customerservice@hogrefe-
                publishing.com
EUROPE: Hogrefe Publishing, Merkelstr. 3, 37085 Göttingen, Germany
                Phone +49 551 99950-0, Fax +49 551 99950-425; E-mail publishing@hogrefe.com

SALES & DISTRIBUTION
USA: Hogrefe Publishing, Customer Services Department,
                30 Amberwood Parkway, Ashland, OH 44805
                Phone (800) 228-3749, Fax (419) 281-6883; E-mail customerservice@hogrefe.com
UK: Hogrefe Publishing c/o Marston Book Services Ltd, 160 Eastern Ave.,
                Milton Park, Abingdon, OX14 4SB, UK
                Phone +44 1235 465577, Fax +44 1235 465556; E-mail direct.orders@marston.co.uk
EUROPE: Hogrefe Publishing, Merkelstr. 3, 37085 Göttingen, Germany
                Phone +49 551 99950-0, Fax +49 551 99950-425; E-mail publishing@hogrefe.com

OTHER OFFICES
CANADA: Hogrefe Publishing, 660 Eglinton Ave. East, Suite 119-514, Toronto, Ontario, M4G 2K2
SWITZERLAND: Hogrefe Publishing, Länggass-Strasse 76, CH-3000 Bern 9

Hogrefe Publishing
Incorporated and registered in the Commonwealth of Massachusetts, USA, and in Göttingen, Lower Saxony, Germany

Printed and bound in the USA

ISBNs: 978-0-88937-404-1 (print), 978-1-61676-404-3 (pdf), 978-1-61334-404-0 (epub)
http://doi.org/10.1027/00404-000

Table of Contents

1

Description

This book focuses on autism spectrum disorder (ASD), which is considered a lifelong neurodevelopmental disorder, qualitatively different from other behavioral disorders that are the foci in this series. As a neurodevelopmental disorder, ASD arises very early in life, often has associated biological and medical conditions, and is not easily treated. In fact, although clearly some individuals improve over time and even "remit," it is considered controversial even today to discuss a "cure" for the disorder.

While ASD comprises persisting and impairing social communication deficits and the presence of restricted and repetitive behaviors and interests, it is much more than that, given the inherent and necessary, evolution-driven social tendencies and proclivities of human nature. Lacking basic skills and motivations regarding socialization leads to the inability to engage in and benefit from many of the activities of life that require such skills: learning, conversing, and engaging in meaningful and mutually beneficial relationships among them.

The following work, beginning with an introduction to old and new classifications of the disorder, explores the parameters of ASD as a heterogeneous condition with associated conditions. The book goes into depth about the complexities of making the diagnosis and differentiating ASD from other related disorders, and describes the state of the science and practice with respect to treating associated features and ultimately the core symptoms of the disorder.

1.1   Terminology

The terminology for ASD relates to its associated conditions and the diagnostic classification of the disorder developed through the *Diagnostic and Statistical Manual for Mental Disorders* (DSM) and *International Classification of Diseases* (ICD) classification systems. A few key abbreviations that are used throughout the book are described in the box below.

Key Abbreviations

AAC	Augmentative and alternative communication
ABA	Applied behavior analysis
ASD	Autism spectrum disorder
DTT	Discrete trial training
EIBI	Early intensive behavioral intervention
EST	Empirically supported treatments
FBA	Functional behavioral assessment
PDD-NOS	Pervasive developmental disorder, not otherwise specified
PRT	Pivotal response treatment
RRB	Restricted, repetitive patterns of behavior, interests, or activities
SCD	Social communication disorder

The terminology for ASD has changed several times since the condition was first introduced as a mental disorder in the 1980s, and most recently it has changed with the publication of the *Diagnostic and Statistical Manual for Mental Disorders,* 5th edition (DSM-5; American Psychiatric Association [APA], 2013). The diagnostic classification has changed from autistic disorder (or autism) to autism spectrum disorder (ASD), and ASD is defined with criteria very similar to the previous criteria for autistic disorder (or autism), pervasive developmental disorder, not otherwise specified (PDD-NOS), and Asperger's disorder, under DSM-IV (APA, 2000). The main changes between the DSM-IV and DSM-5 conceptualization and criteria are the following:

1. The broad diagnostic category is termed *autism spectrum disorder* (rather than the previously termed *pervasive developmental disorder*).
2. ASD is one diagnosis, with specific distinctions for autism vs. PDD-NOS vs. Asperger's disorder (as well as Rett syndrome and childhood disintegrative disorder) removed from the DSM, although these terms are still used clinically and are defined in other classification systems.
3. Within ASD, one domain for social communication deficits is now described (merging the separate criteria for reciprocal social interaction deficits and communication deficits).

In addition, key terms in ASD relate to concepts of the restricted, repetitive behavior domain. In this area, symptoms are now described to include fixated patterns of interests (also described as circumscribed interests or preoccupations) and stereotyped movements (which may include repetitive or idiosyncratic movements). The DSM-5 also includes criteria for hypersensory and hyposensory sensitivities, previously not part of the diagnostic criteria.

Level of support indicators:
Requiring support
Requiring substantial support
Requiring very substantial support

The description of relevant terminology relating to ASD also includes wording for how DSM-5 diagnoses are described more generally. Instead of using a multiaxial system, the DSM-5 uses specifiers, which are descriptors used in the diagnosis to more comprehensively describe an individual. The specifiers for ASD include indication of cognitive functioning (with or without intellectual impairment); language level (with or without language impairment); associations with known medical, genetic, or environmental factors; and classifications that may be used to describe severity for the two criteria domains, categorized by three levels of support. These levels of support are described as requiring support, requiring substantial support, and requiring very substantial support, and these may be used to track change over time within an individual. Separate specifiers are used to describe severity for each domain (social communication deficits and restrictive, repetitive behavior). As such, while some of the specifiers (e.g., association with a medical illness) may be static for individuals, other specifiers may be modified for individuals as they change developmental stage or potentially respond to treatment.

While DSM-5 included the aforementioned changes, the current ICD-10 classifications remain similar to the DSM-IV conceptualizations, as shown in Table 1 (see http://apps.who.int/classifications/icd10/browse/2010). In addition to classifications for autism (childhood autism), other childhood disintegrative disorder, Rett syndrome, and Asperger's syndrome, the ICD-10 system includes an atypical autism classification, for individuals with onset after the age of 3 years. It also includes subthreshold criteria such that a diagnosis of autism may be ruled out. While the ICD-11 revision is not due to be published until 2015, it remains to be seen how and whether these two classifications systems will realign with respect to ASD.

Table 1
DSM-5 and ICD-10 Diagnostic Criteria for ASD

DSM-5	ICD-10
Autism spectrum disorder (299.00) A. Persistent deficits in social communication and social interaction across multiple contexts, as manifested by the following, currently or by history: 1. Deficits in social-emotional reciprocity 2. Deficits in nonverbal communication behaviors used for social interaction 3. Deficits in developing, maintaining, and understanding relationships Specify current severity: severity is based on social communication impairments and restricted, repetitive patterns of behavior B. Restricted, repetitive patterns of behavior, interests, or activities, as manifested by at least two of the following, currently or by history: 1. Stereotyped or repetitive motor movements, use of objects, or speech 2. Insistence on sameness, inflexible adherence to routines, or ritualized patterns of verbal or nonverbal behavior	**Pervasive developmental disorders** **Childhood autism (F84.0)** A. Presence of abnormal or impaired development before the age of 3 years, in at least one out of the following areas: 1. Receptive or expressive language as used in social communication 2. The development of selective social attachments or of reciprocal social interaction 3. Functional or symbolic play B. Qualitative abnormalities in reciprocal social interaction, manifest in at least one of the following areas: 1. Failure adequately to use eye-to-eye gaze, facial expression, body posture, and gesture to regulate social interaction 2. Failure to develop (in a manner appropriate to mental age, and despite ample opportunities) peer relationships that involve a mutual sharing of interests, activities and emotions 3. A lack of socioemotional reciprocity as shown by an impaired or deviant response to other

Table 1 (continued)

DSM-5	ICD-10
3. Highly restricted, fixated interests that are abnormal in intensity or focus 4. Hyper- or hypo-activity to sensory input or unusual interest in sensory aspects of the environment Specify current severity: severity is based on social communication impairments and restricted, repetitive patterns of behavior C. Symptoms must be present in the early developmental period (but may not become fully manifest until social demands exceed limited capacities, or may be masked by learned strategies in later life) D. Symptoms cause clinically significant impairment in social, occupational, or other important areas of current functioning E. These disturbances are not better explained by intellectual disability (intellectual developmental disorder) or global developmental delay. Intellectual disability and autism spectrum disorder frequently co-occur; to make comorbid diagnoses of autism spectrum disorder and intellectual disability, social communication should be below that expected for general developmental level	people's emotions; or lack of modulation of behavior according to social context, or a weak integration of social, emotional, and communicative behaviors C. Qualitative abnormalities in communication, manifest in at least two of the following areas: 1. A delay in, or total lack of, development of spoken language that is not accompanied by an attempt to compensate through the use of gesture or mime as alternative modes of communication (often preceded by a lack of communicative babbling) 2. Relative failure to initiate or sustain conversational interchange (at whatever level of language skills are present) in which there is reciprocal to and from responsiveness to the communications of the other person 3. Stereotyped and repetitive use of language or idiosyncratic use of words or phrases 4. Abnormalities in pitch, stress, rate, rhythm, and intonation of speech D. Restricted, repetitive, and stereotyped patterns of behavior, interests, and activities, manifest in at least two of the following areas: 1. An encompassing preoccupation with one or more stereotyped and restricted patterns of interest that are abnormal in content or focus; or one or more interests that are abnormal in their intensity and circumscribed nature although not abnormal in their content or focus 2. Apparently compulsive adherence to specific, nonfunctional routines or rituals

Table 1 (continued)

DSM-5	ICD-10
	3. Stereotyped and repetitive motor mannerisms that involve either hand or finger flapping or twisting, or complex whole body movements
	4. Preoccupations with part-objects or nonfunctional elements of play materials (such as their odor, the feel of their surface, or the noise or vibration that they generate)
	5. Distress over changes in small, nonfunctional details of the environment
	E. The clinical picture is not attributable to the other varieties of pervasive developmental disorder; specific developmental disorder of receptive language (F80.2) with secondary socioemotional problems; reactive attachment disorder (F94.1) or disinhibited attachment disorder (F94.2); mental retardation (F70-F72) with some associated emotional or behavioral disorder; schizophrenia (F20) of unusually early onset; and Rett's syndrome (F84.2)
	Atypical autism (F84.1)
	A. Presence of abnormal or impaired development at or after age 3 years (criteria as for autism except for age of manifestation)
	B. Qualitative abnormalities in reciprocal social interaction or in communication, or restricted, repetitive, and stereotyped patterns of behavior, interests, and activities (criteria as for autism except that it is not necessary to meet the criteria in terms of number of areas of abnormality)
	C. The disorder does not meet the diagnostic criteria for autism (F84.0)

Table 1 (continued)

DSM-5	ICD-10
	Rett's syndrome (F84.2) A. Apparently normal prenatal and perinatal period and apparently normal psychomotor development through the first 6 months and normal head circumference at birth B. Deceleration of head growth between 5 months and 4 years and loss of acquired purposeful hand skills between 6 and 30 months of age that is associated with concurrent communication dysfunction and impaired social interactions and appearance of poorly coordinated/unstable gait and/or trunk movements C. Development of severely impaired expressive and receptive language, together with severe psychomotor retardation D. Stereotyped midline hand movements (such as hand wringing or washing) with an onset at or after the time that purposeful hand movements are lost **Other childhood disintegrative disorder (F84.3)** A. An apparently normal development up to the age of at least 2 years. The presence of normal age-appropriate skills in communication, social relationships, play, and adaptive behavior at age 2 years or later is required for diagnosis B. A definite loss of previously acquired skills at about the time of onset of the disorder. The diagnosis requires a clinically significant loss of skills (and not just a failure to use them in certain situations) in at least two out of the following areas: 1. Expressive or receptive language 2. Play 3. Social skills or adaptive behavior 4. Bowel or bladder control 5. Motor skills C. Qualitatively abnormal social functioning, manifest in at least two of the following areas:

Table 1 (continued)

DSM-5	ICD-10
	1. Qualitative abnormalities in reciprocal social interaction (of the type defined for autism)
	2. Qualitative abnormalities in communication (of the type defined for autism)
	3. Restricted, repetitive, and stereotyped patterns of behavior, interests, and activities including motor stereotypies and mannerisms
	4. A general loss of interest in objects and in the environment
	D. The disorder is not attributable to the other varieties of pervasive developmental disorder; acquired aphasia with epilepsy (F80.6); elective mutism (F94.0); schizophrenia (F20-F29); Rett's syndrome (F84.2)
	Asperger's syndrome (F84.5)
	A. A lack of any clinically significant general delay in spoken or receptive language or cognitive development. Diagnosis requires that single words should have developed by 2 years of age or earlier and that communicative phrases be used by 3 years of age or earlier. Self-help skills, adaptive behavior, and curiosity about the environment during the first 3 years should be at a level consistent with normal intellectual development. However, motor milestones may be somewhat delayed, and motor clumsiness is usual (although not a necessary diagnostic feature). Isolated special skills, often related to abnormal preoccupations, are common, but are not required for diagnosis
	B. Qualitative abnormalities in reciprocal social interaction (criteria as for autism)
	C. An unusually intense circumscribed interest or restricted, repetitive, and stereotyped patterns of behavior, interests, and activities (criteria as for autism; however, it would be less usual for these to include

Table 1 (continued)

DSM-5	ICD-10
	either motor mannerisms or pre-occupations with part-objects or nonfunctional elements of play materials) D. The disorder is not attributable to the other varieties of pervasive developmental disorder; schizotypal disorder (F21); simple schizophrenia (F20.6); reactive and disinhibited attachment disorder of childhood (F94.1 and F94.2); obsessional personality disorder (F60.5); obsessive-compulsive disorder (F42) **Pervasive developmental disorder, unspecified** This is a residual diagnostic category that should be used for disorders which fit the general description for pervasive developmental disorders but in which a lack of adequate information, or contradictory findings, means that the criteria for any of the other F84 codes cannot be met

Note. ASD = autism spectrum disorder.
DSM-5 criteria reprinted with permission from the *Diagnostic and Statistical Manual of Mental Disorders, Fifth Edition.* © 2013, American Psychiatric Association. All Rights Reserved. ICD-10 criteria reprinted with permission from the *ICD-10 Classification of Mental and Behavioural Disorders Diagnostic Criteria for Research*, pp. 197–201, © 2010 World Health Organization.

1.2   Definition

Deficits in social communication, including reciprocal social interaction, and the presence of restricted, repetitive patterns of behavior, interest, or activities (RRBs) are the defining symptoms of ASD. The onset of these symptoms must be present in early development, the symptoms must cause impairment in several areas of functioning, and the symptoms must not be better explained by intellectual disability or global developmental delay (APA, 2013).

Social communication deficits are among the first concerns reported by parents (Lord, 1995) and have long been considered to be at the core of ASD. Studies have indicated that reduced eye contact, reduced/atypical affect (Clifford & Dissanayake, 2008), poor response to name, and reduced use of communicative gestures are among the earliest indicators of ASD (Osterling, Dawson, & Munson, 2002). Other impairments in this domain include deficits in social-emotional reciprocity (e.g., reciprocal conversation, sharing of inter-

> Social communication deficits are among the earliest indicators of ASD

ests) and impairments in nonverbal communication (e.g., eye gaze, gestural communication, facial expressions of emotion). Deficits in the maintenance of social relationships, difficulties adjusting behavior to different contexts, lack of imaginative play skills, and impairment in, or lack of, peer relationships are also defined as social communication deficits.

RRBs are also core symptoms of the disorder. These behaviors manifest as stereotyped and repetitive motor movements, such as hand flapping, spinning, repetitive use of objects, lining up toys, repetitive speech, and engaging in delayed echolalia. Insistence on sameness, inflexibility with regard to routines, and ritualized speech and behavior are also considered RRBs. Unusual attachment to objects, and hyposensitivity or hypersensitivity to sensory stimuli are also subsumed under this category of behaviors (APA, 2013). While some of these behaviors are observed in typical development, as well as in other psychiatric and genetic disorders, differences in patterns and frequencies have been observed in individuals with ASD compared with other groups (Bodfish, Symons, Parker, & Lewis, 2000).

To meet diagnostic criteria for ASD, an individual must either currently or by history, meet criteria for all three of the symptoms in the social communication domain, and must meet criteria for at least two of the RRBs, also either by current status or history. In addition, impairments in these two domains must affect current functioning. Symptoms also cannot be better explained by intellectual disability or global developmental delay. It is important that developmental (mental) age and age-appropriate norms are considered when determining the extent of impairment, as some symptoms occur at later stages of development (e.g., in peer relationships), and other behaviors can be observed in typical development (e.g., hand flapping).

Diagnosing ASD: Symptoms must cause current impairment Symptoms cannot be explained by intellectual disability or global delay

ASD can be reliably diagnosed in children as young as 24 months, through to adulthood. Diagnostic differentiation, especially both in the very young and in adult populations, can be difficult for many reasons. In early childhood, other developmental delays can be misdiagnosed as ASD, and in older individuals, the reliance on retrospective information regarding early development can be an impediment. See Early Warning Signs and FIRST WORDS Project in Appendix 1.

While the aforementioned criteria define ASD as one diagnostic entity, the presentation can differ substantially across individuals due to variability in core and associated symptoms (e.g., age, cognitive functioning, language ability). These facts impact the use of the term *spectrum* in the diagnosis. This heterogeneity has been observed since the disorder was first characterized by Leo Kanner, and can make diagnosis, understanding of trajectory, and targeting of treatment difficult.

The characteristic heterogeneity in the syndrome was not fully captured in the DSM-IV categorizations. Thus, distinct categories were collapsed into one diagnosis in DSM-5. Further, the PDD-NOS criteria in DSM-IV were vague to the extent that it allowed for a relatively heterogeneous group of children to be represented by this diagnosis. Specifically, DSM-IV diagnostic criteria for PDD-NOS were not precise and allowed for subthreshold symptoms in any one or more of the three core symptom domains (i.e., reciprocal social interaction, and/or communication deficits, and/or presence of RRB) and did not require communication deficits and/or RRB to meet criteria.

If significant RRBs (even by history) are present, a diagnosis of SCD is excluded

It is not yet known if and how the DSM-5 diagnostic criteria will affect prevalence rates of ASD, and how individual diagnoses will be made in practice. Field trial data indicated that many individuals previously diagnosed with autism will meet the criteria, as well as those diagnosed with Asperger's disorder and PDD-NOS (Regier et al., 2013). However, the addition of social communication disorder (SCD) in the DSM-5 may also contribute to changes in diagnostic approach. SCD is defined by difficulties with pragmatic aspects of communication, and includes impairments in the social use of language. However, if significant RRBs (even by history) are present such that a child meets full criteria for ASD, a diagnosis of SCD is excluded. Thus, some individuals diagnosed with PDD-NOS in DSM-IV (who did not have significant symptoms of repetitive behavior and restricted interests) may fall under the new SCD category, while others may fall under the ASD category.

1.3   Epidemiology

Prevalence rates of ASD are reported to be increasing, with several studies indicating alarming rate surges. In this section we will provide a brief overview of the epidemiology of ASD, and discuss some of the challenges that impede epidemiological research in ASD.

1.3.1   Prevalence Rates of ASD

The prevalence rate for ASD in the US is slightly more than 1% and has been increasing

In epidemiological studies across the globe, rates of ASD have ranged broadly. According to the US Centers for Disease Control and Prevention, the current prevalence rate of ASD in the US population was most recently reported to be approximately 11.3 in 1,000 children, or 1.13 % (MMWR, 2012). A study in South Korea reported the highest rates thus far, with prevalence reported to be 2.64 % overall, including 3.74 % in males and 1.47 % in females (Kim et al., 2011). Rates in other parts of Asia have varied from as low as approximately 1 % in China (Sun et al., 2013), to approximately 1.81 % in Japan (Kawamura, Takahashi, & Ishii, 2008). Across Europe, overall rates are reported to be approximately 1 % of the population. While incidence (number of new cases) of the disorder is not well measured and has not necessarily increased, the prevalence rate (total number of cases) has appeared to increase over the past few decades.

Factors Affecting Prevalence Rates
Several factors have influenced the change in prevalence rate, including case ascertainment, case identification, and diagnostic substitution. These issues are important to discuss as they demonstrate how changes in diagnostic criteria, improvements in early identification, and methods of identification can influence case ascertainment and thus estimation of prevalence. Studies have generally used two approaches to case ascertainment: (1) a single-stage method involves reviews of service provider databases and national registries; (2) a multistage method uses record reviews as well, but prevalence is determined by use

of a screening tool or diagnostic checklist. For studies that use screening tools, the sensitivity of the screening tools used is of utmost importance. Due to their nature and intended use, screening tools and methods used to confirm diagnoses in epidemiological studies are vulnerable to, and generally are unable to correct for, the presence of both false positives and false negatives in the population.

Case Identification

The diagnostic criteria for ASD have changed over the years, and as it relates to studies of ASD epidemiology, the broadening of the definition of ASD has likely been related to more identification of cases, and a consequent "rise" in prevalence. As the definition of ASD has broadened, awareness of the disorder has increased, and estimates of prevalence have increased. To exemplify this relationship, one review of epidemiology studies reported a positive correlation between prevalence rate and year of study publication (Fombonne, Quirke, & Hagen, 2011).

Diagnostic Substitution

The potential that diagnostic substitution – the change from one diagnosis to another diagnosis over time – has occurred plagues epidemiological studies in ASD. In ASD, this may relate to children who were initially diagnosed with other disorders such as anxiety disorders or intellectual disability, but as diagnostic criteria or diagnostic processes have changed, they may have later been diagnosed with ASD. Conversely, for children who were previously diagnosed with ASD, but who changed or improved over time, an ASD diagnosis may no longer be appropriate. As the field moves toward improving diagnostic evaluations for young children, it is possible that increasing percentages of children with ASD will show instability in diagnosis, which will have implications for prevalence rates.

Demographic Trends

ASD is approximately four times more prevalent in males than females. This trend has been repeatedly observed across epidemiological studies over the years. There is some evidence that females with ASD are disproportionately more likely to be diagnosed with comorbid intellectual disability, compared with males. Additionally, sex differences in overall symptom severity have not been consistently found (Zwaigenbaum et al., 2012); however, certain types of symptoms and the timing of the identification of symptoms differ by sex (Begeer et al., 2013).

ASD is four times more prevalent in males than females

Several hypotheses have been offered for the sex differences observed in the disorder. Recent studies have postulated that females may have sex-linked protective factors that result in decreased prevalence compared with males; further, affected females may have more risk factors than males (Robinson, Lichtenstein, Anckarsater, Happe, & Ronald, 2013).

Racial, Ethnic, and Socioeconomic Status Findings

In general, racial, ethnic, and socioeconomic status (SES) differences in overall diagnosis of ASD have not been found. However, despite the push for early identification, in the United States, communities often differ significantly regarding the age of diagnosis and the extent of the services received. In the United States, children with lower SES, children from racial and ethnic minorities, and children living in rural communities have a later age of diagnosis, and thus receive intervention services later. In the United States, African American and Hispanic children were reported to be diagnosed 1.5 years later on average than White children (Mandell, Listerud, Levy, & Pinto-Martin, 2002). A review of medical records further confirmed this finding, indicating that children who were African American, Hispanic, and Asian, despite meeting criteria for an ASD, had fewer documentations of a previous ASD diagnosis than White children (Mandell et al., 2009). This disparity in timing of diagnosis also extends to the types of follow-up and subspecialty services received; diagnosis and treatment for comorbid symptoms were reported to be significantly lower in minority populations in the United States (Broder-Fingert, Shui, Pulcini, Kurowski, & Perrin, 2013).

Racial, ethnic, and SES differences in overall diagnosis of ASD have not been found

Several reasons for the disparity in timing of diagnosis have been put forth, with accessibility to services being the front-runner. Early diagnosis in the United States has been promoted because of the benefits of early intervention. However, in some communities, intervention services are either unavailable or difficult to access. Race, ethnicity, and SES can impede identification of ASD and the ability to receive services, resulting in case ascertainment bias in epidemiological studies, which can affect estimates of prevalence. Studies using national registries are limited to families who are in the registry; thus, individuals with limited access to services may remain unidentified.

In the United States and globally, the influence of culture may also result in later identification. Different cultures have a different understanding and expectations of both developmental milestones, and mental health disorders (Grinker, Yeargin-Allsopp, & Boyle, 2011). Further, a main impetus for early identification has been the effect of early intervention; in countries without this type of service infrastructure, it is arguable that the need for early identification may not be as well highlighted.

Another factor that researchers will have to explore is how the course of the disorder affects prevalence rates. Early diagnosis and early intervention can lead to improved outcomes for individuals, and for some, significant reductions in symptoms. See Appendix 1 for a link to the Centers for Disease Control and Prevention website.

1.4   Course and Prognosis

The course and prognosis of ASD are as heterogeneous as its initial presentation. Characterized as a neurodevelopmental disorder, ASD when diagnosed implies impairment throughout the lifespan, and the majority of individuals with ASD maintain this diagnosis as they age (Lord et al., 2006). The symptom presentation has been examined both cross-sectionally and longitudinally; longitudinal studies provide a context for better understanding current functioning, approaches to intervention, and the trajectory of ASD. In this section, what is known about the stability of the disorder over time, and predictors that lead to positive prognosis, will be reviewed. Understanding the course and prognosis for ASD is complicated by the varying presentations of the disorder, and the presence of associated symptoms.

1.4.1   Trajectory of ASD

Core Symptoms

Overall symptom severity is reported to remain generally stable for the majority of individuals, with a minority displaying either improving or worsening symptoms (Gotham, Pickles, & Lord, 2012). However manifestations of the symptom clusters are more likely to change over time, and several different trajectories, both in terms of pace and quantity, have been identified. For example, communication impairments and social symptoms may be more likely to improve rapidly compared with repetitive behaviors (Fountain, Winter, & Bearman, 2012). In a study examining longitudinal changes on the Autism Diagnostic Interview–Revised (Rutter, LeCouteur, & Lord, 2003a), both social interaction and communication scores were reported to improve significantly in young children over the course of 2 years. In some individuals, interest in social interactions was reported to improve in early adolescence (McGovern & Sigman, 2005). Repetitive behaviors were reported to decrease in some populations of children over longer periods of time (Richler, Huerta, Bishop, & Lord, 2010). In contrast, over shorter time periods, and despite improvements in other areas of impairment, these behaviors remain relatively stable (Lord, Luyster, Guthrie, & Pickles, 2012).

Trajectory of Associated Symptoms

There is a very strong relationship among core symptoms of ASD, cognitive ability, and verbal skills. The trajectory of cognitive skills has not been clearly established, with some studies reporting a decline in cognitive skills over time, although this finding may be due to difficulties in measurement of cognitive skills over the course of development (McGovern & Sigman, 2005). The trajectory of language development in ASD has also only been looked at minimally, as very few studies have followed children over long periods of time. One study that followed children through age 9 indicated that language development appears to have several different trajectories, dependent on cognitive abilities, joint attention skills, and symptom severity; over 24 % developed some language (verbal but not fluent), and an additional 25–50 % used fluent language (Anderson et al., 2007). Over the course of 2 years, another study found that verbal IQ increases were reported in children and adolescents who had overall improvements in core symptoms (Gotham et al., 2012).

> There is a strong relationship among core symptoms of ASD, cognitive ability, and verbal skills

Adaptive Behavior

The course of many areas of functioning for individuals with ASD is entangled in the severity of the core and associated symptoms – for example, adaptive behavior is one such area of functioning. In one longitudinal study following individuals into adulthood, while adaptive behaviors improved from childhood to adolescence, greater adaptive gains were associated with a higher level of functioning in early social engagement and cognitive ability (McGovern & Sigman, 2005). In a study of children first diagnosed at 2 years of age, and later evaluated at 9 years, improved adaptive social and communication skills were predicted by earlier language development, nonverbal IQ, and symptoms (Charman et al., 2005). In another example, children whose core symptoms either remained stable or worsened over time had adaptive skills in the area of daily living that also worsened with age (Gotham et al., 2012).

Trajectory Into Adulthood

Few adults with ASD live independently

Similar to studies of childhood and adolescence, those in adults with lower cognitive functioning early in development and greater severity of symptoms have shown them to have poorer outcomes, and they may even develop more behavioral and psychological problems. Social difficulties, academic difficulties, and unemployment are common in adult populations with ASD; additionally, few of these individuals live independently (Eaves & Ho, 2008). See Case Vignette 1 for an example of transition for a young adult.

Case Vignette 1

Transition Planning for a Young Adult With ASD

Gina is an 18-year-old woman who was diagnosed with ASD at the age of 4 years. Soon after her diagnosis and up to the age of 10 years, Gina received applied behavior analysis therapy, speech therapy, and occupational therapy, both at school and privately. At the age of 16, Gina was prescribed risperidone, which her parents reported was done to address symptoms of irritability. For this evaluation, Gina was seen at an autism clinic with her parents. Gina's parents expressed concern regarding the next appropriate educational and vocational steps for Gina. Gina was just about to graduate from a high school in which she received individualized educational support and was enrolled in a learning support program that teaches independent living skills.

Evaluation of current ASD symptoms indicated continued social and communication impairments, as manifested by difficulty in engaging in reciprocal conversations, inconsistent and abnormal use of eye contact, and reduced use of gestures and facial expressions. Difficulty engaging with peers was also reported. Parents reported that up to the age of 12 years, Gina engaged in significant repetitive behaviors, including repetitive motor mannerisms (brief hand flapping), stereotyped language (repeating phrases she had heard, out of context), and difficulty with changes in routines. At the time of evaluation, her parents reported that her motor mannerisms were no longer evident, and while her stereotyped language had decreased significantly, when upset, she still repeated phrases she had heard, and she could sometimes be overheard speaking to herself using coping strategies that she had been taught. According to her parents, Gina was better able to tolerate changes but might "talk to herself" to calm down when unexpected changes occurred. However, her parents reported that Gina continued to show circumscribed interests. Currently, she shows an intense interest in transportation (e.g., subways, trains) spending considerable amounts of time looking up maps and schedules. Current testing has also indicated mild intellectual ability, and mild impairments in adaptive behavior, indicating a comorbid mild intellectual disability.

Several recommendations were outlined including building a transition plan for when Gina ages out of the school system at age 21. According to recent studies, the first 3 years following transition from secondary school represent a virtual "cliff" when individuals with ASD are at great risk for social isolation, limited activity, and limited engagement in activities outside of the home. With this in mind, Gina's parents were provided with several recommendations that ideally would have been started at age 14. Gina would begin the process of applying for disability support services. In addition, Gina's parents were starting a consultation with legal support services to develop a plan for Gina's future welfare. It was recommended that she would also benefit from an educational program that focused on maximizing the development of Gina's practical living skills. Gina would also begin a vocational evaluation program to assess her interests and establish education and vocational goals.

Because the greatest predictor of employment in adult years for individuals with disabilities is employment during secondary school, it was also recommended that Gina begin volunteer and internship programs. Ideally, these programs would be related to her areas of interest and would be provided with the support of transition-age services to help her and the workplace adapt to her individual needs. To support this goal, Gina's parents found her a volunteer position providing tours (with assistance) at the transportation museum. Gina's primary tour guides and the museum staff required some initial education and training, but because of their familiarity with the population, they were accommodating of Gina's idiosyncratic habits. In addition, they learned strategies to prompt Gina when she engaged in extended monologues during tours or spoke too loudly. Gina was also instructed on how to go to a "safe place" to take a break when she became overwhelmed or anxious, but she still often required reminders from members of the museum staff as well.

Predictors of Outcome

Outcome research in ASD has examined varying domains and constructs. Increased cognitive performance, decreased symptom severity, change in diagnosis, increased adaptive skills, and independent living are all examples of variables that have been studied. In this section, unless otherwise specified, we define *outcome* as improvements in overall symptom presentation.

Similarly to initial presentation of ASD, both the core and associated symptoms can affect its trajectory. Conversely, the severity of core symptoms can affect outcomes in associated areas, such as language (Thurm, Lord, Lee, & Newschaffer, 2007). Studies consistently report that individuals with higher cognitive functioning have better long-term outcomes (Howlin, Goode, Hutton, & Rutter, 2004), and better response to treatment (Howlin, Magiati, & Charman, 2009), while individuals with lower cognitive functioning remain generally stable. One study found that children with higher nonverbal IQ and less severe social impairment and repetitive behaviors were more likely to change diagnostic category (Lord et al., 2006).

Core and associated symptom severity can affect the trajectory of ASD

Similarly, stronger language ability and adaptive functioning have been associated with better outcomes in later life. Children who develop language before the age of 5 years are reported to have better functioning in several domains (Howlin et al., 2004). The age of first words also has a demonstrated relationship with cognitive functioning and adaptive ability, as children who developed initial language later may also have lower cognitive functioning and adaptive skills compared with children with earlier emerging language (Mayo, Chlebowski, Fein, & Eigsti, 2013).

Predictors of improved outcome: Language ability Adaptive skills Higher nonverbal IQ

It is important to mention that the role early intervention (and intervention in general) plays in outcome is complicated based on the relationships described above, and may depend on the timing and frequency of intervention. Studies have indicated that, in general, better outcomes are associated with early intervention, and specific types of early intervention support such improvements (Dawson et al., 2010).

Optimal Outcome in ASD

A minority of individuals diagnosed with ASD have achieved an *optimal outcome*. This term refers to individuals previously diagnosed with ASD who no longer meet the diagnostic criteria. Predictors of optimal outcome in ASD are similar to predictors of symptom improvement – that is, higher cognitive ability and receptive language skills are the positive predictors. One of the differences observed – less severe social impairments in the early years is characteristic of individuals with optimal outcome. Other studies have found small, but significant pragmatic and semantic language differences in children previously diagnosed with ASD who show significant improvement (Kelley, Paul, Fein, & Naigles, 2006). However, as the authors of these studies note, *optimal outcome* defined by lack of diagnosis of ASD at a later time point does not necessarily imply lack of impairment in other areas, and further exploration of the psychiatric, academic, and vocational status of individuals in this group is needed.

Overall, the course and prognosis of ASD circle around several recurrent themes: severity of symptoms, cognitive function, language ability, and adaptive behavior. Frequently, the role of cognitive functioning serves as an intermediary variable for changes in ASD. These findings can help clinicians target certain areas for intervention, and predict the types of supports individuals with ASD will most benefit from. See Appendix 1 for a list of unique abilities observed in some individuals with ASD.

2

Theories and Models of ASD

In the *Diagnostic and Statistical Manual of Mental Disorders*, 5th Edition (DSM-5; APA, 2013), ASD is characterized as a neurodevelopmental disorder, indicating that the behavioral symptoms, manifestations, and indicators of the disorder are neurological and developmental in origin. Categorization as a disorder described as neurodevelopmental reflects current thinking from the vast research that has been conducted in the last 4 decades regarding the etiology of the disorder. In the past, beginning in the 1940s, psychiatric, psychoanalytic, and biological models have all been used to describe ASD.

2.1   Early Theories and Models of ASD

2.1.1   Leo Kanner

The behavioral symptoms of ASD were first described by the Austrian psychiatrist Leo Kanner. In 1943, Kanner used the terminology *autistic disturbances of affective contact* to describe the behaviors he observed in 11 pediatric patients. Kanner noted that the disorder was probably present from birth, and was marked most prominently by social impairment, which he postulated was the symptom that most distinguished autism from other disorders. This social impairment was present along with communication impairment and the presence of repetitive behaviors.

Leo Kanner, an Austrian psychiatrist, first described autism and its behavioral symptoms

Social impairment, or "autistic aloneness," was defined as a desire to be alone, detachment from others, and an inability to relate to others. Parents had reported that this symptom was present in early development, as the children he described did not use anticipatory gestures to be picked up, nor did they nestle when held. Impairment in the communicative use of language was also noted in this cohort. Kanner later summarized that 3 of the 11 children did not develop language, and 8 had articulation difficulties, pronominal reversal, echolalia, and stereotyped language (Kanner & Eisenberg, 1955). The symptoms of restricted and repetitive behaviors and interests were defined as desire for sameness, ritualistic behaviors, always following "the same prescribed course," and using exactly the same language and actions, repetitive play with objects, including spinning objects, and a "fascination" with objects. Around the same time that Kanner was observing these symptoms in his patients, the Viennese physician Hans Asperger noted similar symptoms in a group of male children in Germany. He reported the presence of social interaction deficits and stereotyped behaviors, which he termed "autism," but noted that in this group of children, communication and cognitive impairments were absent (Asperger & Frith, 1991). As the conceptualization of ASD expanded, it was the absence of communicative and cognitive impairments that differentiated Asperger's disorder from autism.

2.1.2   Psychoanalytical Perspective

Although Kanner believed that biological factors might be responsible for autism, he also believed that parenting practices played a part in the development of this disorder, describing the parents of his patients as aloof and cold, and noting that these parents had obsessive tendencies. As has since been noted (Baker, 2010), this claim slowed any understanding of the disorder and damaged both children and families. In 1967, psychologist Bruno Bettelheim described mothers of children with ASD as "refrigerator mothers"; by withholding affection from their children, these mothers caused autism (Bettelheim, 1967). Deficits in parenting skills were also highlighted as the cause of autism in several other studies, with difficulties ranging from communication skills to the structure of the home environment (Behrens & Goldfarb, 1958; Clerk, 1961). Fortunately, these theories were not supported by studies; clinical observations demonstrated no differences in the parenting skills and parental warmth of parents of children with ASD and non-ASD controls (e.g., Cox, Rutter, Newman, & Bartak, 1975).

2.1.3   Biological Models

In the 1960s and 1970s, biological theories of ASD began to emerge, and findings from related studies helped to further rebuke psychoanalytic theories of ASD. Early biological theories included theories of the disorder as an organic brain disease, and specifically suggested that damage to the brain during the prenatal period and/or during birth caused the disorder. The reticular system was implicated by two groups of researchers with contrasting views, one seeing ASD as an underactivity and the other as an overactivity of the system (Rutter, 1968). Extensive exploration of the molecular underpinnings of ASD began in the 1980s. Although the brain has been the primary focus, molecular theories of ASD have often used a systems approach, vs. an organ-specific approach, to uncovering the etiology of ASD. Dysfunction and inflammation of the immune system (Pardo, 2007), damage to brain cell tissue (Vargas et al., 2005), gene–environment interactions (Chaste & Leboyer, 2012), and mitochondrial problems (Shao et al., 2008) have all been examined in relation to the ASD genotype and phenotype. These studies have uncovered abnormalities in brain tissue and cerebrospinal fluid (Pardo, Vargas, & Zimmerman, 2005), but require replication before firm conclusions can be drawn.

Early biological theories considered autism an organic brain disease

Some studies have misattributed or overemphasized the role of biological factors in ASD. For instance, while early estimates of the role of genetic factors suggested that in approximately 25 % of ASD cases, Fragile X was comorbid, later estimates were lower. Among the most damaging misattributions was a much publicized but subsequently retracted study ascribing the cause of at least some cases of ASD to specific vaccinations (Murch et al., 2004). Like the damaging effect of early psychoanalytic theories of ASD, this speculation, based on discredited research, negatively influenced understanding of the etiology of the disorder, and has yet to be proven.

2.1.4   Neurological Bases of ASD

Recognition of neurological factors associated with the disorder also emerged in the 1960s and 1970s when the presence of seizures was reported in early ASD cases (Creak & Pampiglione, 1969). Similarities in onset of ASD and epilepsy were noted, and as research in this area progressed, links to other disorders characterized by abnormal epileptiform activity, such as tuberous sclerosis, were reviewed (Pampiglione & Moynahan, 1976). The relationship between epileptiform activity and the presence of intellectual disability, as well as language delays, further highlighted connections with ASD. Neuroimaging studies have been integral to understanding the functional and structural aspects of the brain in ASD. Underconnectivity and abnormal connectivity between brain regions (Minshew & Keller, 2010), structural abnormalities, and brain volume differences (Hadjikhani, Joseph, Snyder, & Tager-Flusberg, 2006) have been some of the most illuminating findings.

Neurological theories of ASD:
Abnormal brain connectivity
Structural abnormalities

2.1.5   Social, Cognitive, and Neuropsychological Theories

While not necessarily etiological in the sense of explaining the biological mechanism of disease ontogeny, neuropsychological theories have been extensively used to describe the psychological and developmental pathways that "cause" neurodevelopmental derailment in ASD. While many such theories have been explored, few have become well established or widely accepted. In the 1970s and 1980s, the social impairments in ASD were linked to the neuropsychological concept, theory of mind (ToM). ToM refers to the ability to understand and predict behavior in another individual – in other words, engage in social cognition. Early theories postulated that ASD was due to an absence in this cognitive mechanism, which thereby affected the ability to interact, play, and engage in reciprocal conversation. There were, however, limitations regarding the ability of the theory to describe the basis of the repetitive behaviors observed in ASD (Frith, 1996); furthermore, ToM abilities can be taught and often develop later in children. Currently, ToM theorists have shifted focus from a postulated global deficit of ASD to a focus on using these concepts to understand earlier occurring social processes, such as joint attention, and their relationship to ASD (Rutter, 2011).

Theory of mind:
The ability to understand and predict the behavior of others is impaired in ASD

Related theories include social motivation theory (Dawson, Meltzoff, Osterling, Rinaldi, & Brown, 1998), and detail-focused cognitive style (Frith, 1989). The social motivation theory suggests that impairments in the ability to orient to, and receive reward from, social stimuli are at the core of ASD. According to this theory, early in development, typically developing children demonstrate preferences for socially motivating stimuli that lead to patterns of behavior of which the primary goal is maintaining social interactions; these behaviors in turn lead to the development of social communication skills. However, for children with ASD, the biological and neurological networks needed for these early social tasks are impaired, and these early impairments result in social communication impairments and preferential interest in non-social stimuli. Like the ToM account of ASD, however, this theory fails to account for the presence of repetitive behaviors in the disorder (Chevallier, Kohls, Troiani, Brodkin, & Schultz, 2012).

Detail-focused cognitive style, or weak central coherence, was put forth by Frith (1989) as an explanation of some of the impairments observed in ASD. The theory centered on how individuals with ASD processed the environment, and it suggested that while typically developing individuals are able to perceive objects in the environment as a whole, or as a coherent structure, this skill was less developed and "weak" in ASD. As a result, individuals with ASD attend to more details in the environment, and to nonsocial aspects of the environment, which according to the theory accounts for impairment in social cognition, and sensory sensitivities (Happe & Frith, 2006). Early findings, however, have been inconsistently corroborated in later studies with more heterogeneous groups.

2.1.6   The Recent Past: ASD Classification

ASD classification now considers autism as a spectrum disorder

Two of the leading classification systems of disorders and diseases – the DSM and the ICD – have in part utilized classification schemas that mirrored research and understanding of ASD at specific points in time. In the DSM-II (APA, 1968), although Kanner believed the disorders to differ, ASD was classified under childhood schizophrenia. Almost 10 years later, the ICD-9 (World Health Organization [WHO], 1977) officially recognized the symptom clusters of ASD as infantile autism. In 1980, the third edition of the DSM (APA, 1980) introduced the category of pervasive developmental disorders, and also included the diagnostic category of infantile autism. The revision of the manual included a terminology change from infantile autism to autistic disorder (APA, 1987), and an additional diagnosis, PDD-NOS, was defined. The PDD-NOS diagnosis included individuals who showed some, but not all, of the impairments associated with autistic disorder. In 1992, the 10th revision of the ICD (WHO, 1993) included the category of pervasive developmental disorders in its classification system.

In the DSM-IV (APA, 1994), ASD continued to be characterized, under the umbrella term of pervasive developmental disorders, as autistic disorder, and disorders with similar symptoms, Rett syndrome, and Asperger's disorder were included under the pervasive developmental disorders rubric. A diagnosis of Asperger's disorder was given to individuals with social impairments and repetitive behaviors, without a history of language and cognitive delays or impairments in most areas of adaptive behavior. Although Rett syndrome and childhood disintegrative disorder were classified as pervasive developmental disorders, different patterns of onset for these disorders, and the known genetic etiology associated with Rett syndrome (the mutation in the methyl CpG–binding protein 2 [MeCP2] gene), differentiated them from autistic disorder, Asperger's disorder, and PDD-NOS. As such, due to the similar presentation of symptoms, the last three disorders were commonly referred to as autism spectrum disorders.

While biomedical models have illuminated the genetic, neurological, and biological underpinnings of ASD, the behavioral model continues to be at the core of a diagnosis, and determining the best way to classify the behavioral symptoms has been challenging. As reflected in the classification of ASD in the DSM-5, research regarding the social and communication deficits have indicated that these deficits are intertwined. Across all domains, the heterogeneity of, and relationship among, symptoms makes classification difficult (Lord & Jones, 2012).

As noted, the DSM-IV criteria for PDD-NOS resulted in a broad diagnostic category which made reliability, classification, and comparison challenging. Another diagnostic challenge involved the differentiation between autistic disorder and Asperger's disorder. Studies have found few core symptom differences between individuals diagnosed with autistic disorder who have average to above-average cognitive functioning, and individuals with Asperger's disorder, suggesting that diagnostic differentiators are not based on core impairments, but rather on associated features such as cognitive functioning and communication impairment. A study comparing diagnostic practices across sites had similar findings – differences in diagnostic practices were not related to symptom presentation, but rather to associated features (Lord, Petkova, et al., 2012).

The categorization of ASD will likely continue to change. Advances in genetic and neurobiological models, and their role in the behavioral phenotype of the disorder will undoubtedly influence the understanding, classification, assessment, and treatment of ASD.

3

Diagnosis and Treatment Indications

As biological markers have not yet been identified, ASD continues to be defined behaviorally. Accurate diagnosis is important for determining the appropriate interventions and identifying the supports the individual and family will need. As we learn more about the trajectory of ASD, the initial diagnostic process may aid in identifying the types of challenges individuals may experience as they age, and give insight into prognosis.

When assessing ASD, beyond the range of presentation of the core symptoms, a clinician must also consider the effects of factors such as age, cognitive functioning, language level, and adaptive behavior. The presence of comorbid disorders such as anxiety disorders, attention deficit/hyperactivity disorder (ADHD), and genetic disorders can complicate diagnosis. The combination of variable core symptoms and diverse functioning necessitates that a diagnostic evaluation be comprehensive, including an observation of symptoms; a caregiver report of symptoms; evaluation of functioning in cognitive, receptive and expressive language, motor, and adaptive areas; and an assessment of comorbid disorders. Feedback in diagnosing ASD should include a careful discussion of all of these elements in context (see Clinician's Guide to Providing Effective Feedback in Appendix 1).

3.1 Assessment of Core Symptoms

The assessment of core ASD symptoms should be multidimensional and involve a combination of caregiver report and behavioral observation of symptoms. As individuals with ASD may have different presentations of symptoms in different environments, using several methods in conjunction provides a diagnostic picture of the symptoms across settings, a history of symptom presentation, and current symptoms and concerns. Two broad categories can be used to describe the types of measures used to assess ASD symptoms (see box below): (1)

Assessing ASD

Screening measures
• Completed by parents/caregivers

Diagnostic measures
• Administered by trained professionals
  – Direct observation
  – Parent report

screening measures, or first-level diagnostic tools, and (2) diagnostic measures, or second-level diagnostic tools. Each of these methods was designed with specific aims, and as such assesses symptoms differently.

3.1.1   Screening Measures

Screening measures can be categorized by their intended use by parents or caregivers, or by professionals. Parent/caregiver screening measures generally serve the purpose of screening large populations, and are designed to quickly determine whether or not an individual has specific behaviors, or a developmental profile that warrants further evaluation. Parent/caregiver screening measures tend to be easy to use, are generally rating scales, and are cost-effective. Screening measures developed for use by professionals are designed to further screen at-risk populations – that is, children identified as having delayed or abnormal development (e.g., language delays, social communication delays, etc.), and generally include rating scales, observations, and brief interviews. These tools are often referred to as part of Stage 2 screening, tend to take longer to administer, and often require some level of training.

Heterogeneity in ASD:
Core symptoms
Age
Cognitive functioning
Language level
Adaptive behavior

The Social Responsiveness Scale (SRS; Constantino & Gruber, 2005), the Social Communication Questionnaire SCQ (SCQ; Rutter, LeCouteur, & Lord, 2003b), and the Modified Checklist for Autism in Toddlers (M-CHAT; Robins, Fein, Barton, & Green, 2001) are among the most frequently used caregiver screening tools for ASD. All three measures are used as a caregiver report of symptoms, but differ in the age group they target, as well as in psychometric sophistication. The SCQ is based on the Autism Diagnostic Interview–Revised (ADI-R; Rutter, LeCouteur, & Lord, 2003a) and has been validated for individuals with ASDs who have a mental age of 18 months into adulthood, although sensitivity was reported to be better in individuals 8 years and older (Corsello et al., 2007). The SRS questionnaire is strongly correlated with the ADI-R, and was developed in part to distinguish ASD populations from non-ASD populations. Both measures have been reported to have reduced sensitivity with individuals with lower cognitive functioning (Charman et al., 2007; Hus, Bishop, Gotham, Huerta, & Lord, 2013). The M-CHAT (Robins et al., 2001) is a modification of the Checklist for Autism in Toddlers (CHAT; Baron-Cohen, Allen, & Gillberg, 1992).The M-CHAT includes caregiver questions, and targets children age 16 months to 30 months. See Appendix 1 for a link to the M-CHAT.

3.1.2   Diagnostic Measures

Diagnostic measures are developed for use by trained professionals and are used to confirm diagnosis (see box below). These tools usually require intensive training to be used effectively, and they tend to be either parent/caregiver interview–based or based on behavior observation. The current gold standard diagnostic tools are the ADI-R (Rutter et al., 2003a) and the recent revision to the Autism Diagnostic Observation Schedule (ADOS; Lord et al., 2000), the Autism Diagnostic Observation Schedule-2 (ADOS-2, Lord, Rutter, et

---

Diagnostic Measures

- Parent interviews, e.g., Autism Diagnostic Interview-Revised (ADI-R), and Diagnostic Interview for Social Communication Disorders (DISCO)
- Observation-based instruments, e.g., Autism Diagnostic Observation Schedule, 2nd Edition (ADOS-2), and Childhood Autism Rating Scale (CARS)

---

al., 2012). The ADI-R is a semistructured parent or caregiver interview of both historical and current symptoms in the core areas of ASD. Used for both adults and children, the ADI-R implements a diagnostic algorithm based on the DSM-IV criteria for ASD. The Toddler ADI-R version of the measure was recently developed for use in children as young as 12 months up to the age of 47 months (Kim & Lord, 2012).

The ADOS-2 is a semistructured observation that varies in form based on age and language level. Recently adapted from the ADOS, the measure now includes five modules, a toddler module, for children as young as 12 months and up to 30 months (or when phrase speech is present), one module for individuals with phrase speech, one for individuals over 30 months with less than phrase speech, and two modules for fluent speakers. The toddler versions of both the ADOS-2 and the ADI-R have adapted questions and tasks accounting for different levels of language and behaviors that are associated with younger children – for example, an assessment of the quality and frequency of babbling (consonant-vowel reduplications); additionally, the Toddler ADI-R has questions regarding the age of onset for some behaviors.

The Childhood Autism Rating Scale (CARS; Schopler, Reichler, & Renner, 1988) is a semistructured interview used to assess ASD behaviors in children. It assesses behaviors across 14 domains, a 15th domain is used to rate overall impressions. Domains are rated on a scale of 1 to 4, with higher scores indicating more impairment. A total score of 30 and under indicates the individual is not on the autism spectrum, scores between 30 and 36.5 indicate mild to moderate ASD, and scores 37 to 60 indicate severe ASD. One of the weaknesses of the CARS is its low specificity in young children. The Diagnostic Interview for Social Communication Disorders (DISCO; Wing, Leekam, Libby, Gould, & Larcombe, 2002) is a semistructured caregiver interview of an individual's developmental history and current functioning. Unlike the ADI-R, which focuses on ASD symptoms, the DISCO includes assessment of other psychiatric symptoms and developmental concerns. See Table 2 for several of the different types of measures used to assess ASD symptoms.

Table 2
Screening and Diagnostic Tools for ASD

Measure	Assessor	Description (measure type; number of items; length of administration)	Population (age group)	Symptoms assessed
Screening				
Autism Spectrum Quotient (AQ)	Parent/Caregiver	Questionnaire; 50 items scored on a Likert-type scale	> 16 years	Current presentation of core symptoms
Autism Spectrum Screening Questionnaire (ASSQ)	Parent/Caregiver	Questionnaire; 27 items scored on a point scale; 10 min	School-aged children with ≥ mild intellectual disability	Current presentation of core symptoms; associated symptoms
Checklist for Autism in Toddlers (CHAT)	Parent/Caregiver and clinician	Questionnaire, observation; 9 parent questions, 5 clinician items	18 months	Current presentation of core symptoms
Communication and Symbolic Behavior Scales–Developmental Profile (CSBS-DP)				
Infant Toddler Checklist	Parent/Caregiver	Screening questionnaire; 24 items; 5–10 minutes	12–24 months	Current presentation of core symptoms; language and gesture use

Table 2 (continued)

Measure	Assessor	Description (measure type; number of items; length of administration)	Population (age group)	Symptoms assessed
Caregiver Questionnaire	Parent/Caregiver	Questionnaire; 15–25 min	12–24 months	Current presentation of core symptoms; language and gesture use
Behavior Sample	Clinician	Semistructured observation; 20–30 min	12–24 months	Current presentation of core symptoms; language and gesture use
Early Screening of Autistic Traits Questionnaire (ESAT)	Parent/Caregiver	Questionnaire; 14 items scored as a yes/no	14 months	Current presentation of core symptoms
Gilliam Autism Rating Scale (GARS)	Parent/Caregiver	Questionnaire; 42 items	3–22 years	Presentation of core symptoms; developmental history
Infant Toddler Checklist (ITC)	Parent/Caregiver	Questionnaire; 24 items	6–24 months	Social communication; language; motor development
Modified Checklist for Autism in Toddlers (M-CHAT)	Parent/Caregiver	Questionnaire; 23 items in a yes/no format	16–30 months	Current social communication skills

Table 2 (continued)

Measure	Assessor	Description (measure type; number of items; length of administration)	Population (age group)	Symptoms assessed
Pervasive Developmental Disorder Behavior Inventory (PDDBI)	Parent/Caregiver Teacher	Questionnaire; 124 to 188 items	18 months to 12 years, 5 months	Current presentation of core symptoms; aggression; learning and memory
Social Communication Questionnaire (SCQ)	Parent/Caregiver	Questionnaire; 40 items scored with a yes/no	4–40 years	History and current core symptoms
Social Responsiveness Scale (SRS)	Parent/Caregiver Teacher	Questionnaire; 65 items scored on a Likert-type scale; 15 to 20 minutes	4–18 years	Current presentation of core symptoms
Diagnostic				
Autism Diagnostic Interview– Revised (ADI-R)	Clinician	Semistructured caregiver/parent interview; 93 items; 90–180 minutes	4–90 years of age	History and current core symptoms
Toddler Autism Diagnostic Interview–Revised (Toddler ADI-R)	Clinician	Includes additional 32 items assessing onset and early communication skills	12–47 months; mental age of 10 months	History and current core symptoms
Autism Diagnostic Observation Schedule (ADOS)	Clinician	Semi-structured behavioral observation; 30–60 min	24 months to 90 years of age	Current presentation of core symptoms

Table 2 (continued)

Measure	Assessor	Description (measure type; number of items; length of administration)	Population (age group)	Symptoms assessed
Autism Diagnostic Observation Schedule, 2nd Edition (ADOS-2)	Clinician	Semi-structured behavioral observation; 30–60 min	12 month to 90 years of age	Current presentation of core symptoms
Childhood Autism Rating Scale (CARS)	Clinician	Structured observation; 15 items; 20–30 min	> 2 years	Current presentation of core symptoms
Diagnostic Interview for Social and Communication Disorders (DISCO)	Clinician	Semistructured caregiver interview; 362 items; 120–240 min	All ages	Core symptoms; developmental level; daily living skills
Screening Tool for Autism in Two-Year-Olds (STAT)	Clinician	Interactive observation; scored as pass/fail; 20 min	24–36 months	Social communication skills; imitation skills
Developmental, Dimensional and Diagnostic Interview (3Di)	Clinician	Semistructured caregiver interview; 266 ASD items; additional items to assess comorbidity; 90–180 min	3–18 years	History and current core symptoms; comorbid symptoms, parent demographics

3.2   Assessment of Associated Symptoms

3.2.1   Cognitive Functioning

Frequently used as a predictor of later outcomes, an assessment of cognitive functioning should be a core component of an ASD evaluation. Cognitive functioning has been used to characterize individuals as either "high-functioning" or "low functioning," but more importantly (and appropriately), a cognitive assessment allows the clinician to contextualize the impairments observed in ASD. As noted, several symptoms (e.g., language, peer relationships, repetitive behaviors) require evaluation in the context of developmental level, and cognitive assessment allows for this comparison.

> **Cognitive functioning assessment is critical in contextualizing ASD symptom presentation**

In ASD, cognitive functioning is associated with symptom presentation – for example, in some individuals, lower cognitive functioning is associated with more frequent and different types of RRBs, and greater impairments in social communication skills. Also of note, specific cognitive profiles are observed in ASD (Munson et al., 2008), with individuals demonstrating higher nonverbal development, compared with verbal development; this profile has been theorized to be characteristic of the ASD phenotype. Furthermore, many measures have decreased diagnostic validity in children with lower cognitive functioning. The ADOS shows significantly higher specificity in children with at least an 18-month mental age (Risi et al., 2006); thus, for individuals with severe cognitive impairment, certain measures may not be appropriate, or at least should be used with extreme caution.

Overall, an assessment of the cognitive functioning of an individual with ASD can aid in accurate diagnosis, help determine strengths and weaknesses, and assist in the development of appropriate interventions. However, due to the impairments associated with ASD – such as difficulties with motivation, difficulty staying on task, repetitive interests in objects, and language impairment – assessment of cognitive functioning may be challenging. Using a developmental approach to cognitive assessment is critical – choosing the appropriate measures, implementing breaks, and using appropriate motivators (Ozonoff, Goodlin-Jones, & Solomon, 2005).

3.2.2   Language Functioning

The assessment of receptive and expressive language skills is a core component of an ASD evaluation. Specific language profiles are also common in ASD, with receptive language tending to be worse than expressive language. While receptive and expressive language skills are generally assessed as part of the cognitive evaluation, a language evaluation provides further information regarding an individual's overall functioning. There is also significant evidence that at least a subset of individuals with ASD also meets criteria for specific language impairment (Leyfer, Tager-Flusberg, Dowd, Tomblin, & Folstein, 2008) or has language processing or fluency difficulties, necessitating assessment for differential diagnosis and treatment planning.

> **Assessment of receptive and expressive language skills is a core component of an ASD evaluation**

The range of language abilities observed in ASD is vast. In both nonverbal and verbal children, assessing the propensity for use of language is necessary. For children with verbal abilities, language impairments may range from scripted speech to difficulty with reciprocal conversation. Using additional language measures – for example, an expressive vocabulary test – may highlight where a verbal child has difficulty. Producing speech-like vocalizations may be difficult for some children, and structural impairments may contribute to these language difficulties.

3.2.3   Adaptive Functioning

Adaptive functioning is another important component of the ASD evaluation. Beyond cognitive assessment, a measurement of adaptive skills provides information on how an individual functions on a day-to-day basis. In terms of treatment planning, an evaluation of adaptive functioning can offer insight into possible strengths and weaknesses. Profiles observed in ASD include weaknesses in social and communication skills, and adaptive skills that are lower than overall cognitive functioning (Charman et al., 2011).

3.2.4   Comorbid Disorders and Symptoms

Because an individual with an ASD diagnosis may be impaired across several domains, the clinical manifestations of comorbid disorders may appear differently, or may be disguised; conversely, the presence of the comorbid disorder can mask ASD symptoms, resulting in delayed diagnosis. The first step in assessing comorbid disorders requires that the clinician identify how the coexisting disorder affects the individual. An assessment of associated factors is the second step. This assessment needs to focus on developmental changes, as some comorbid disorders may not present until an individual is older. Likewise, certain types of learning disorders are usually identified in school-aged children, thus these disorders would inevitably be missed in preschool-aged children.

Clinically assessing and treating comorbidity, particularly psychiatric comorbidities, can improve intervention outcome; however, for many reasons, including overlap in the symptoms of some disorders, there are few measures that accurately assess comorbid symptoms in ASD. Available measures may provide an assessment of a specific symptom domain (e.g., irritability, anxiety). In choosing a measure to assess comorbidity, it is important to carefully examine specific response patterns to rule out the possibility of overreporting, underreporting, or misattributing specific symptoms.

A functional behavioral assessment (FBA) can be used to identify targets for behavior therapy

In addition to standardized measures, behavioral assessment procedures are often used to identify causes, develop interventions, and measure change from treatment for both core symptoms and associated maladaptive behavior problems. Using a behavioral therapy framework, a functional behavioral assessment (FBA) can be used to identify targets for behavior therapy. Information is collected on common *antecedents and consequences* associated with a behavior in FBAs. The results of FBAs provide hypotheses about the situations and conditions that predict the when, where, and why a problem behavior may occur. The FBA will also provide hypotheses regarding functions of a problem behavior, and subsequently allow the clinician to develop interventions based on these hypotheses.

3.3   Assessment in the Presence of Multiple Disabilities

Individuals with multiple disabilities are often in need of a diagnostic evaluation, and determining the best approach to assessment is complex, demanding both skill and awareness of the strengths and weaknesses of diagnostic measures. This topic is becoming more important in ASD diagnosis, given that there are individuals reported to be diagnosed with ASD with conditions such as cerebral palsy, and sensory impairments, including vision and hearing impairments. As with any comorbid disorder, sifting out the effects of the comorbid impairment vs. ASD symptoms is indicated, and in the case of multiple disabilities, the impact these impairments have on overall clinical presentation has to be determined. Core symptoms may be masked by these impairments, and vice versa. For example, assessing eye contact with individuals with vision impairments, or delayed language for someone with hearing impairments, can be complicated and requires that the clinician thoroughly assess the breadth of the impairment. In many cases, the measures routinely used for ASD assessment are not standardized for populations with multiple disabilities and require a minimum level of ability in some areas (e.g., the administration of the ADOS-2 requires that the examinee is able to walk independently).

3.4   Assessment of Change

Among the biggest challenges for the ASD research community, and quite different from initial diagnostic assessment, is the assessment of change in symptoms. As best practices in early identification of ASD continue to develop rapidly, and interventions and treatments are utilized and explored, the challenge of how to assess change over time becomes magnified. Commonly used measures were developed primarily as diagnostic tools, and use of these tools as outcome measures is not advised. Currently, few standardized measures have enough sensitivity to examine the changes that can occur over a short period (≤ 12 months) for a child with ASD.

Few standardized measures of ASD have enough sensitivity to assess change that occurs in < 12-month periods

The Pervasive Developmental Disorders Behavioral Inventory (PDDBI; Cohen et al., 2003) is among the few measures developed to examine change. The PDDBI categorizes behavior as adaptive/maladaptive and approach/ withdrawal. One of the drawbacks of the measure is that it was validated in a sample of children who did not receive standardized diagnostic assessments of ASD symptoms. Recently, new diagnostic algorithms for the ADOS were developed and implemented in the ADOS-2, with the goal of assessing individual severity and therefore potentially change in social affect and restricted and repetitive behaviors. Serving as a measure of severity, a comparison score (also known as a calibrated severity score) can be derived using these new algorithms. Calibrated severity scores have been shown to be consistent over a short period of time (Shumway et al., 2012) and require further testing for measuring improvement.

The development of children with ASD can be as variable in presentation as the disorder, and assessment should be approached as a continuous process. The presentation of the disorder changes as individuals age, develop skills, and respond to interventions, and it is essential to determine the current impact of core symptoms and associated symptoms. In addition, it is critical for the clinician to consider all comorbid factors, rule out differential diagnoses, and determine the impact of comorbid disorders.

3.5   Differential Diagnosis

Beyond the difficulties associated with the valid assessment of the core symptoms of ASD are consideration of several other variables that are not specific to core ASD symptoms, but which affect presentation and can lead to misdiagnosis. Some of these include cognitive functioning, language functioning, other behavioral problems, and age of diagnosis.

3.5.1   Cognitive Functioning

The impact of cognitive functioning on ASD symptom presentation has been repeatedly documented. As noted in Section 3.2.1 Cognitive Functioning, cognitive impairment can affect symptom presentation within ASD; due to the overlap in symptom presentation, significant cognitive impairment can also lead to misdiagnosis.

Developmental factors, such as age, can affect how cognitive impairment presents

Cognitive impairment infrequently appears without other behavioral symptoms, and the presence of cognitive impairment, along with associated symptoms that often overlap with ASD, can lead to a misdiagnosis. One example of an associated symptom seen in individuals with intellectual disability is repetitive behaviors; individuals with significant impairments in cognitive functioning often display repetitive behaviors. In non-ASD adults (Bodfish et al., 2000) and in non-ASD toddlers (Medeiros, Kozlowski, Beighley, Rojahn, & Matson, 2012), impaired cognitive functioning is related to an increased presence of repetitive behaviors. Developmental factors such as age can also affect how cognitive impairment presents; a longitudinal study indicated that toddlers with significant cognitive impairment were frequently misdiagnosed with ASD (Lord, 1995). Simply put, the presence of these behaviors in conjunction with cognitive impairments is not necessarily indicative of an ASD diagnosis, making it imperative to consider the role of cognitive impairment when assessing for ASD.

3.5.2   Language Functioning and Communication Disorders

Expressive language level at earlier ages is a predictor of outcome

Communication impairments are among the first concerns reported by parents of children with ASD; expressive language level at earlier ages is a dependable predictor of outcome in individuals with ASD (Mayo et al., 2013). However, these impairments are not diagnostically specific, and, in young children, are not in themselves conclusive predictors of ASD. It is for this reason that the criterion of language delay without compensation was removed from the DSM-5 criteria for ASD.

Specific language impairment (SLI) is a disorder marked by impairment in the structural language aspect of communication; in many cases, associated social communication impairments are also present. Pragmatic language impairment (PLI) is characterized by impairments in the social use of language, symptoms that often align with the social communication symptoms that are observed in ASD. These symptoms include difficulties with recognizing and responding appropriately to social cues, and difficulty engaging in "small talk"; individuals with pragmatic language impairment however, are reported to have subtle differentiators in their presentation of social communication deficits, as well as repetitive behaviors (Reisinger, Cornish, & Fombonne, 2011). The addition of SCD in the DSM-5 allows for a specific diagnosis to be made for individuals with such impairments in verbal and nonverbal communication for social use, who do not meet criteria for ASD.

> Pragmatic language impairment is characterized by impairments in the social use of language

> Specific language impairment is marked by impairment in the structural language aspect of communication

3.5.3 Developmental Delays

Developmental delays, such as those captured under the overarching term *global developmental delay,* may be particularly difficult to differentiate from ASD, especially when diagnosed in young children, due to the overlap of symptoms. As earlier diagnosis of ASD is becoming more prevalent, there is a potential risk of misdiagnosing developmental delays that are not ASD. Currently, further assessment is recommended if reaching milestones is delayed in the areas of communication (babbling, single words, phrase speech) or there is a loss of social skills; however, delays in these areas can be associated with several types of developmental delays.

Defined by significant delay in at least two areas of functioning (e.g., gross motor, fine motor, speech or language, cognition), the term *global developmental delay* captures by design several types of developmental disorders, and the presentation of these delays is not easily differentiated from that of ASD. However, the underlying cause and trajectory may differ; for example, children with ASD have a different pattern and rate of language acquisition, as well as different rates of acquisition of social skills, compared with children with developmental delays. A system of "red flags" has been developed to help differentiate ASD from non-ASD delays in young children (Wetherby et al., 2004). The symptoms highlighted include response to names and showing things of interest to others. More recently, a review by Mitchell et al. (2011) indicated several symptoms that differentiate children with ASD from those with other developmental delays at 12 months, 18 months, and 24 months of age (see Table 3).

Table 3
ASD Discriminators in Young Children

Discriminator	12 months	18 months	24 months
Decrease in response to name	X		
Quality of facial expressions	X		X
Decreased quantity of facial expression	X	X	
Decreased positive affect			X
Decreased use of social gaze	X	X	X
Impaired gaze switching		X	
Decreased interest in peers			X
Decreased shared enjoyment			X
Adaptive communication			X
Gesture use		X	X
Atypical use of objects	X		
Repetitive movements: Posturing			X
Repetitive play with objects			X

Based on review by Mitchell et al. (2011).

3.5.4   Other Psychological Disorders

Beyond associated features that may lead to misdiagnosis, there are specific psychiatric disorders that need to be ruled out, for example ADHD and anxiety disorders such as obsessive-compulsive disorder (OCD).

Attention Deficit/Hyperactivity Disorder

The behavioral profile, as well as the neurobiological and genetic underpinnings of ADHD, overlaps with ASD. With respect to the behavioral profile, social impairments are frequently observed in individuals with ADHD, and when present in young children, the presence of such social impairments presents a challenge for accurate diagnosis. Children with ADHD experience peer rejection, have difficulty with peer interactions, and find it difficult to maintain peer relationships. Overall social incompetence has also been reported. Neuropsychological and neuroimaging studies have indicated that executive functioning impairments exist in these children, and impairment in the frontostriatal region has been demonstrated in both disorders (Gargaro, Rinehart, Bradshaw, Tonge, & Sheppard, 2011). Despite these similarities, behavioral, and neuropsychological factors do differentiate the disorders. The nature of the social impairments tends to differ: Children with ADHD are reported to be

The behavioral profile, neurobiological substrate, and genetic underpinnings of ADHD overlap with ASD

disruptive during play, frequently interrupting conversations (Abikoff et al., 2002). Children with ASD demonstrate more difficulty shifting attention and planning than individuals with ADHD (Bramham et al., 2009).

Obsessive-Compulsive Disorder
Although repetitive behaviors are at the core of both ASD and OCD, the presentation of these behaviors is qualitatively and quantitatively different. OCD is generally characterized by obsessions and compulsions; in contrast, a broader range of repetitive behavior is observed in children with ASD. Children with OCD have more compulsions than children with ASD (Zandt, Prior, & Kyrios, 2007); in adults, behaviors such as checking and compulsively washing were less likely in ASD (Lewin, Wood, Gunderson, Murphy, & Storch, 2011). This differentiation in symptoms is significant in terms of treatment. The theoretical constructs behind these disorders are different: Repetitive behaviors in OCD are linked to anxiety, but a meaningful link has yet to be unearthed in ASD.

Identifying the similarities and differences among developmental and psychiatric disorders is key to accurate diagnosis across the board; however, in a disorder as complex as ASD, the differentiation between disorders is frequently difficult and can seriously affect the types of services and interventions recommended. Further complicating differential diagnosis is the fact that many disorders can occur comorbidly with ASD, sometimes masking the disorder or exacerbating symptoms.

3.6   Comorbidities and Associated Conditions

The prevalence of comorbid disorders in ASD ranges from approximately 5% to 70%. The variation in estimated comorbidity rates relate to the type of comorbidity reported (e.g., psychiatric vs. genetic), and differences in study methodology. Psychiatric disorders – such as impulse control disorders, anxiety disorders, and depressive disorders – genetic disorders, gastrointestinal problems, and neurological problems, along with sleep problems and epilepsy, are among the most frequently observed.

In ASD, comorbid diagnoses are associated with several factors, such as age, language functioning, and developmental level. Some disorders may be easier to identify if the patient is able to verbalize symptoms (e.g., pain associated with gastrointestinal problems) or to have insight into their behaviors (e.g., depression). Many of the co-occurring conditions thought to affect the presentation of the core deficits in ASD can be further impairing, and are crucial to consider within a clinical context, especially when prioritizing treatments.

3.6.1   Psychiatric and Developmental Disorders

A large population-based study reported that the rate of psychiatric comorbidity in ASD was approximately 10% (Levy et al., 2010). Anxiety disorders such as OCD, and disruptive disorders such as ADHD and oppositional defiant dis-

The rate of psychiatric comorbidity in ASD is not fully understood

ADHD and anxiety disorders are frequently comorbid conditions in individuals with ASD

order, are among the most commonly reported comorbid psychiatric disorders. Depressive disorders and Tourette's disorder are also diagnosed frequently. The rate of some disorders, such as anxiety disorders and ADHD, has been reported to be so high, as well as difficult to distinguish, that in prior versions of the DSM there was an exclusion for diagnosing both ASD and ADHD in the same individual. But given that many of the treatments used frequently in ASD, particularly pharmacological agents, are designed to target symptoms of specific comorbidities (e.g., impulsiveness, aggression), it is important to make a full differential diagnosis for all potential psychiatric comorbidities, and continue monitoring for these disorders over time.

Anxiety Disorders

The presence of a co-occurring anxiety disorder in individuals with ASD can serve to complicate and worsen ASD symptoms. It is estimated that between 11 % and 84 % of individuals with ASD also experience an anxiety disorder; with generalized anxiety disorder, specific phobias, OCD, and separation anxiety disorder reported most commonly (White, Oswald, Ollendick, & Scahill, 2009). Even though high prevalence rates have been reported, it is possible that anxiety disorders may be underreported in ASD. The degree of overlapping symptoms, such as in OCD, may make it difficult for clinicians to determine the extent to which the presence of obsessions and compulsions justifies an additional diagnosis. Further, reporting of anxiety symptoms may be complicated by verbal ability; one study found an inverse relationship between anxiety and communication ability in children with ASD (Davis et al., 2012).

Attention Deficit/Hyperactivity Disorder

The rates of co-occurring ASD and ADHD range from approximately 13 % to 74 %, depending on the sample (population-based vs. clinical). The co-occurrence of the disorder and the overlap in some symptoms is so high that it has been suggested that the disorders may occur on a continuum with bidirectional presentation of symptoms – ASD traits have been observed in children with ADHD (Grzadzinski et al., 2011), and ADHD symptoms observed in ASD. Greater impairment in symptoms has been reported for individuals with comorbid ADHD (Gadow, DeVincent, & Pomeroy, 2006).

Intellectual Disability and Language Disorders

Intellectual disability is the most frequently co-occuring condition in individuals with ASD

Among the developmental disorders, intellectual disability co-occurs in 40 % to 70 % of individuals with ASD, making it one of the most common comorbid diagnoses. The effects of co-occurring intellectual disability in ASD are widespread and pervasive. In addition, intellectual disability highly correlates with some types of comorbid symptoms and disorders observed in ASD, such as epilepsy. Specific cognitive profiles in ASD provide diagnostic leads and can be helpful in differential diagnosis.

Language disorders also have high prevalence rates in ASD. Beyond the language impairments related to the core social communication deficits of an ASD diagnosis, individuals may also present with language problems such as speech apraxia, specific language impairment, and fluency disorders.

Genetic Disorders

Approximately 15% of ASD cases have a known genetic cause (Mendelsohn & Schaefer, 2008). Disorders such as Fragile X syndrome (FXS), tuberous sclerosis, William's syndrome, and disorders with associated chromosomal abnormalities (e.g., 15q11-13, 22q11.2), are well known to co-occur with ASD. Phenotypic variables observed in ASD with known genetic etiologies have been delineated: Muscle weakness, ataxia, behavioral regression, and breathing abnormalities were among the variables listed, which if present, warrant genetic testing (Carter & Scherer, 2013).

Gastrointestinal Disorders

Prevalence rates of co-occurring gastrointestinal disorders (GIDs) in ASD are variable (from 9% to 70%). The difficulties in assessing the prevalence of GID in ASD are related to the impairments caused by the core symptoms, specifically communication impairments. As such, parent report remains the main source of information regarding gastrointestinal distress in children with ASD. Observable problems, such as constipation and diarrhea are more likely to be reported, while symptoms such as stomach cramping are likely to be under-reported and may go undetected. Restrictive diets, picky eating, and medication usage have been identified as causes of GIDs in ASD; a genetic link has also been indicated for a subgroup of individuals (Campbell et al., 2009). The presence of GID may exacerbate behavior problems, food refusal, mealtime difficulty, and tantrums, and must be evaluated in the context of treatment and overall quality of life.

Neurological Disorders

Neurological comorbidities are highly prevalent in ASD, and epilepsy, sleep problems, and motor dysfunction are the most widely reported neurological disorders. Like the comorbid disorders reviewed above, neurological disorders can further complicate the heterogeneity of the ASD phenotype, affecting behavior, symptom presentation, response to intervention, and trajectory.

Epilepsy

Epilepsy occurs at a rate of approximately 30% in ASD. Because some genetic disorders (tuberous sclerosis, FXS) that have high rates of comorbidity with ASD also have high rates for epilepsy, researchers have proposed that the disorders may have similar etiologies (Brooks-Kayal, 2010). The types of seizures observed in ASD have varied, and the age of onset for epilepsy in ASD is reported to be highest at two time points: early childhood at 1 to 5 years of age and adolescence at 11 to 18 years of age (Parmeggiani et al., 2010). A large percentage of epilepsy cases in ASD are reported to co-occur with intellectual disability, and an earlier onset of epilepsy is correlated with more impairment in cognitive functioning and poor developmental outcome. Increased mortality rates of individuals with ASD and comorbid epilepsy have also been reported (Gillberg, Billstedt, Sundh, & Gillberg, 2010).

Epilepsy occurs at a much higher rate than expected in individuals with ASD

Sleep Problems

Difficulty falling asleep (sleep latency) and sustaining sleep (sleep efficiency) are the most commonly reported sleep issues in ASD. An association between

ASD symptom severity and the occurrence of sleep disorders has been observed. The types of sleep difficulties do differ by age, however, and younger children tend to have more behavioral problems associated with sleep (e.g., resistance at bedtime), and more awakenings during the night, while older individuals tend to have more difficulty with sleep latency (Goldman, Richdale, Clemons, & Malow, 2012). In young children, sleep disturbances have been linked with behavioral problems during the day (Sikora, Johnson, Clemons, & Katz, 2012), while in adults, daytime sleepiness and cognitive performance difficulties have been reported. More importantly, sleep problems appear to persist through childhood into adolescence and adulthood in individuals with ASD, and they can affect the ability to learn, emotional regulation, and behavior.

Sleep problems are frequently reported and difficult to manage in individuals with ASD

Motor Impairments

Motor functioning has been recognized as an issue in ASD since the initial characterization of the disorder. While repetitive motor behaviors are a core component of the disorder, delayed motor milestones and motor disorders have also been reported to occur comorbidly. Gross and fine motor impairments, apraxia, gait problems, and motor planning problems are reported motor issues in this population, and some motor problems can lead to difficulties in other areas of development. For example, oral-motor impairments are frequently related to delays in speech, and fine motor difficulties can lead to impairments in academic and adaptive areas of functioning.

Comorbid medical and psychiatric issues are important in understanding the heterogeneity of the ASD phenotype. Early identification of some types of comorbid issues can lead to earlier diagnosis, and the development of more appropriate treatment interventions for individuals with ASD. See Case Vignette 2 for an example of the diagnostic process and treatment recommendations for a young child with ASD.

Case Vignette 2

Diagnosis and Treatment Recommendations

Eli is a 4-year-and-1-month-old boy whose parents reported concerns with his development. Eli's parents reported that they first became concerned with Eli's development when he was approximately 18 months of age, and he was not talking. Eli began using single words at the age of 27 months, and phrase speech emerged at the age of 43 months. Other developmental milestones (e.g., motor) were achieved on time.

His parents reported that Eli currently communicates by using three- to four-word phrases. His parents reported that Eli generally communicates only to express his needs; however, he also frequently repeats phrases he has heard previously, including phrases he has heard from television shows. He also repeatedly asks the same questions – for example, asking the question "Are you a dog?" to family members and anyone else he meets. His parents said he asks this question at least four times a day. His parents described Eli as having a limited range of facial expressions: happy, sad, and neutral. His parents stated that he sometimes laughs inappropriately; for example, at school he will laugh and it is unclear to his teachers why. Eli's mother reported that his response to the approaches of others is limited, such that he may sometimes smile in response to familiar people, like his parents and teachers, but he does not smile in response to strangers.

Difficulties with transitions were reported, as Eli becomes upset when there are changes in his daily routine, including at school where teacher reports indicate he becomes agitated and hits others if asked to sit in a different seat in the classroom. Eli plays with a limited range of toys (e.g., toy cars, blocks) but at times appears somewhat imaginative (e.g., pushing a toy car and making car sounds). His parents also reported that Eli's interests and activities include several non-functional activities such as twirling pieces of string for up to 30 min at a time. They reported that it is becoming more and more difficult to stop him from this repetitive play.

Eli is currently enrolled in a regular education, private preschool classroom with 16 children, one teacher and one assistant teacher. Concerns have increased since his enrollment, as teachers have noticed an increasing discrepancy between Eli's engagement compared with that of his classmates. In addition to not attending during circle time, he rarely approaches or engages with classmates. If peers approach him, his teacher has stated that he looks at them and may smile, but generally does not respond otherwise. He often seems interested in the textured classroom walls, and will spend considerable time in a corner peering at the wall while he runs his finger over the wall walking back and forth. His mother reported that while he primarily engages in parallel play with siblings, he will sometimes join in some games.

A cognitive evaluation indicated that Eli had significant delays in nonverbal and verbal skills, with nonverbal skills in the 36-month age range, and verbal skills in the 26-month age range. His adaptive functioning was also significantly delayed. An assessment of single-word receptive and expressive language also indicated significant delays.

Module 1 of the ADOS-2 was administered to Eli. During the ADOS-2, Eli generally used phrases when requesting things. He frequently engaged in immediate echolalia, repeating words and phrases the examiner used, and his speech had a high pitch. Eli's use of gestures was limited and included reaching and pointing both to request and to express interest in things. Overall, Eli had limited use of eye contact to initiate and regulate social interactions with the examiner, engaging in eye contact only on one occasion, when requesting a toy from the examiner. He also had a limited range of facial expressions (smiling and grimacing), and did not direct these expressions to the examiner. Eli engaged in play with a few toys, including a cause and effect toy and a toy telephone, saying good-bye when placing the toy telephone down. He also played with toy cars in a repetitive manner, moving a car back and forth while humming. Other repetitive behaviors were observed, as Eli flicked the eyes of a doll and looked closely at the wheels of a toy car when it was moving.

Results of both the parent interview and the behavioral observations indicate that Eli meets all three DSM-5 ASD criteria in the social communication domain, as well as all four criteria in the domain of RRBs. Moreover, these symptoms are causing clinical impairment at school, as he is not benefitting from the instruction given, and not engaging socially as expected. At home, impairment is also evident, as his parents are having a harder and harder time getting him to engage in activities of daily living (e.g., meals, baths). Additionally, Eli's overall cognitive functioning and adaptive functioning is significantly delayed. Eli meets criteria for ASD, with accompanying intellectual impairment. The level of support required for communication is very substantial, and substantial for RRBs.

Given this overall diagnostic presentation, an individualized education plan geared toward children with ASD, intellectual disability, and language impairments is warranted. Such a plan will include some time spent in an "autism" classroom, where a teacher specialized in ASD will work with Eli on academic skills, as well as target social communication deficits and reduction of restricted interests and repetitive behavior. Within this classroom, specific time is designated to work on increasing joint attention skills as well as using established methods to use routines and themes to increase appropriate social overtures and focus specifically on imaginative play. In addition, the plan will include pull-out time for speech therapy and occupational therapy, as well as a group speech therapy session.

Goals for intervention should include increasing use of language across contexts, increasing use of gestures, and integration of eye contact. In addition, Eli needs a comprehensive evaluation with a developmental pediatrician who can conduct a thorough medical history and physical examination to rule in or out further testing for genetic or other medical conditions associated with ASD.

4

Treatments for Core and Associated Symptoms of ASD

4.1 Methods of Treatment

The heterogeneity and developmental nature of ASD necessitates a multidisciplinary approach integrating efforts from medical, mental health, educational, vocational/community, and allied health disciplines (e.g., speech therapy, occupational therapy, music therapy). A long-term perspective is also necessary to provide developmentally sensitive care across the lifespan of an individual with ASD. Treatment targets for young children with ASD typically involve improving functional speech and social engagement, while providing environmental and behavioral supports to manage RRBs. Thus, interventions for most young children are primarily implemented within home- or community-based early childhood programs and may also include services from related service professionals (e.g., speech therapists). Behavioral and emotional problems become a focus for treatment as individuals enter middle childhood. It is during these years that children with ASD may be more likely to receive treatment in mental health or psychiatric clinics to facilitate management of problem behaviors (e.g., irritability/aggression, attention) and anxiety-related symptoms. Families often use complementary and alternative medicine (CAM) treatments as adjuncts to conventional treatments. Throughout the lifespan, medical specialists in fields such as neurology, endocrinology, and gastroenterology are often involved to address associated medical conditions (e.g., epilepsy).

A multidisciplinary approach to treatment is necessary for ASD

Treatment of ASD is complicated by its lifelong course, heterogeneity of symptomatology and comorbid conditions, and most importantly, its developmental and pervasive nature. Individuals with ASD frequently engage in multiple treatments in several domains (e.g., multiple medications and multiple behavioral interventions) simultaneously. Parents report using an average of seven different treatments, with more than half reporting use of speech therapy, other skills-based therapies, behavioral therapies, and medications (Green et al., 2006). This influences clinical care as well as research on the efficacy and effectiveness of treatments.

To date, treatment studies have been limited in their ability to tailor treatments for this heterogeneous, early-emerging developmental disorder. The research approaches reviewed below reflect the current state of the science which, when compared with behavioral sciences research in other childhood psychiatric conditions, is in a relatively nascent stage.

4.1.1   Psychosocial Interventions

Comprehensive ASD programs:
Enroll children at 18–36 months
Treatment provided 25–40 hr per week

Psychosocial interventions are a mainstay in the clinical care of individuals with ASD, and the last 20 years of behavioral intervention research have been marked by significant advances in the early identification and treatment of young children with ASD. Successful interventions have addressed ASD-specific deficits through developmentally anchored, ASD-specific treatment programs which capitalize on the cognitive and learning styles of individuals with ASD. Specifically, *comprehensive programs* are typically considered a first-line intervention for young children. These early education programs typically enroll children aged 18–36 months, involve 25–40 hr/week of treatment, and are delivered by specialized professionals in educational, home-based, or community settings. In addition to comprehensive programs, *focused intervention* programs are also commonly used with children. These focused interventions may include allied health services such as speech therapy, occupational therapy, sensory integration therapy, music therapy, social skills, and physical therapy. Focused or modular programs may also be used to address comorbid symptoms such as anxiety, aggression and disruptive behaviors, and hyperactivity. Despite remarkable advances in the treatment of ASD, remediation of core social impairments in ASD remains a significant treatment challenge.

4.1.2   Pharmacological Treatment Models

At present, no pharmacological treatments are available for core ASD symptom domains

Until recently, medication management of ASD largely relied on adaptation of treatments from other disorders to address associated, but not core features of the disorder. This approach focused on identifying target symptoms, such as irritability/aggression or RRBs, and adapting efficacious treatment models. However, adaptation models have yielded mixed results. Atypical antipsychotics – aripiprazole and risperidone – for the treatment of disruptive behaviors (i.e., irritability) are among the few US Food and Drug Administration (FDA)–approved treatments for symptoms associated with ASD. At present, no pharmacological treatments are available for core symptom domains. Encouraging advances in recent years have investigated novel pharmacotherapy approaches which include translation of mechanisms from genetic findings into therapeutics as well as exploration of novel treatment targets which may influence general states such as learning (e.g., glutamate) and social motivation (e.g., oxytocin).

In addition to psychopharmacological treatments, a variety of medications are used to treat common associated medical conditions in ASD (e.g., sleep, digestion, epilepsy). Families often seek CAM approaches to target ASD symptoms and/or such associated problems during the early childhood years, which may include specialized diet regimens, animal-assisted therapies, and alternative medicines.

4.1.3   Approach to Review of Treatment Methods

Available treatments for individuals with ASD have emerged from several fields including education, psychotherapy, and pharmacology, each with discipline-specific standards for validating interventions. Given the diversity of disciplines that contribute to treatment models for people with ASD, commonly used terms from psychotherapy treatment research (e.g., empirically supported treatments [ESTs]) will not be systematically used in this manual. Nonetheless, the review emphasizes treatments in the empirical literature with the most promise. Many commonly used interventions either have not yet been evaluated or are emerging as evidence-informed approaches; these will also be included. Finally, CAM treatments will be reviewed given their widespread use in ASD.

4.1.4   Comprehensive Treatment Programs for Early Childhood Education

A 2001 report from the National Research Council's Committee on Educational Interventions for Children with Autism recommended the use of comprehensive treatment models in the education of young children with ASD (National Research Council, 2001). Several comprehensive treatments for ASD were included as model programs in that report, and many more have been developed in the past decade. While continued investigation is needed to show efficacy and effectiveness for specific therapies, it is also essential to identify active ingredients of these effective treatment programs. Most evidence-based early childhood programs for young children with ASD share common behavioral and educational strategies including the use of direct instruction, visual supports, and developmentally anchored skill targets. Many of the programs described in subsequent sections have been instrumental in changing educational and behavioral treatment approaches for people with ASD.

Most evidence-based early childhood programs share common behavioral and educational strategies

To put the breadth of comprehensive treatments for ASD into context, Odom et al. (2010) defines "comprehensive treatment models" (CTMs) as consisting of the following:

1. multiple components, including child-centered instruction and a family component;
2. treatment goals and methods that address several developmental domains (e.g., language, behavior, social skills);
3. high-intensity instruction (25–40 hr week, daily, multiple hours/day, across settings); and
4. intervention that occurs over a long period of time (e.g., several months to years).

See Table 4 for a list of commonly used comprehensive treatments for young children with ASD, along with names of specific treatment programs representing each approach.

Applied Behavior Analysis
Applied behavior analysis (ABA) represents a class of comprehensive treatment programs based in well-established learning principles (e.g., classical, operant, and observational). The application of learning theory in the education of people with disabilities has its roots in mid-20th-century educational practices. The framework and growth of the science of behavior analysis for ASD can be attributed to the seminal work of O. Ivar Lovaas. Lovaas used the

Table 4
Comprehensive Treatment Programs for Young Children With ASD

General approach	Brand names associated with approach	Target age groups	Overview of approach	Treatment outcomes supported in literature
Applied behavior analysis	ABA	All ages		
Early intensive behavioral intervention (EIBI)	Lovaas therapy UCLA training model	Toddlers and preschoolers	1:1; 20–40 hr per week, includes specific curriculum implemented through ABC approach	Gains in IQ, adaptive behavior, socialization, communication, and daily living skills
	Discrete trial training (DTT)	All ages	Typically 1:1; use of ABC approach motivated through rewards	Gains in cognitive, communication, social, and behavioral skills
Naturalistic behavior therapy	Pivotal response training (PRT) Nova Scotia model	Preschoolers	Use of core motivational and teaching strategies in naturalistic settings	Decreased behavioral problems; decreased ASD symptoms for children with IQ > 50
Inclusive programs	LEAP, Walden	Preschoolers		Insufficient data
Division Treatment and Education of Autistic and Related Communication-Handicapped Children (TEACCH)		All ages	Use of individualized plans, visual supports, and environmental engineering in structured teaching and parent training	Insufficient data

Table 4 (continued)

Developmental/relationship-based

Developmental, individual difference, relationship-based model	DIR/Floortime	All ages	Parent or therapist led engagement in play, focusing on self-regulation, intimacy, two-way and complex communication, emotional ideas and emotional thinking	Insufficient data
Relationship-development intervention	RDI	All ages	Parent-based systematic treatment using everyday life situations, focusing on emotional referencing, social coordination, declarative language, flexible thinking, relational information processing, and foresight and hindsight	Insufficient data

Social communication interventions

Social Communication Emotion Regulation Transactional Support	SCERTS	All ages	Routines-based intervention in natural environment; individualized curriculum, include parent training and use of transactional supports in inclusive, naturalistic settings	Insufficient data

Integrative models

Early start Denver model	ESDM	Toddlers and preschoolers	Developmentally based curriculum implemented mostly through 1:1 with parents or therapists, emphasizing imitation, nonverbal and verbal communication, and social development	One study showing improvement in IQ, adaptive behavior and autism symptoms

Note. ABA = applied behavior analysis; ABC = antecedent-behavior-consequence; ASD = autism spectrum disorder; LEAP = Learning Experiences: Alternative Programs for Preschoolers and Parents.

basic principles of learning and behavior from operant theory to systematically teach new skills and reduce problem behaviors in children with ASD. As described below, the basic model rests on the behavioral paradigm of antecedents (A), behaviors (B), and consequences (C) (see Figure 1).

Discrete Trial Training

DTT uses the operant techniques of shaping, chaining, modeling in the form of mass, discrete trials

As described in the original report (Lovaas, 1987) and in the several manuals that describe the specific curriculum (e.g., Leaf & McEachin, 1999; Maurice, Green, & Luce, 1996), discrete trial training (DTT) is an educational practice that uses the operant techniques of shaping, chaining, and modeling in the form of *mass, discrete trials* to break down skills and teach each skill to a high level of accuracy. In practice, this model includes treatment "sessions" that typically include a one-on-one ratio of therapist to child. While sessions can be adapted to many situations, they are typically carried out at least some of the time while seated at a table. While the curriculum is quite specific, with targeted behaviors as goals and methods of discrete trials for learning, behaviors that are often taught sequentially include attending behaviors (e.g., sitting, using eye contact), language (e.g., both comprehension of words and production of sounds and words) and preacademic and then academic tasks (e.g., pointing to a picture, letters, or numbers). Adaptive skills such as toileting and dressing are also included in the curriculum. Sessions are organized around a therapist (who can be a professional or a tutor supervised by a behavior analyst) conducting mass discrete trials of specific tasks where the verbal instruction and/or prompts are used as the antecedent, the child responds with a behavior, and the desired consequence for the behavior is a reward, which may be a "tangible" or a social reward. Prompts are decreased until mastery for each behavior is achieved, and generalization and maintenance trials are used when trials move to subsequent and more complex goals.

The original study of this intervention enrolled 49 children under the age of 4 years for approximately 2–3 years. The study used a quasiexperimental,

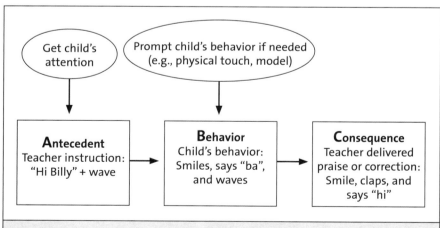

Figure 1
Discrete trial training procedures: antecedent-behavior-consequence (ABC) model used to teach new skills (e.g., teaching a child with ASD to wave good-bye).

nonrandomized design to compare the treatment (40 hr/week of ABA) with two control conditions: < 10 hr/week of ABA and treatment as usual. Results indicated that 47 % of children receiving 40 hr per week of ABA sessions were enrolled in mainstream classroom placement and had average cognitive skills by first grade. In contrast, only 2 % of children from both comparison conditions achieved this outcome. The Lovaas publication (Lovaas, 1987) was the first to provide evidence that the developmental trajectory of people with ASD could be influenced by specific teaching practices.

The original form of behavior modification or ABA used in Lovaas's seminal work has subsequently been known as the UCLA training model, DTT, and more recently, the early intensive behavioral intervention (EIBI). This ABA model has been replicated often. A meta-analysis of over 100 studies suggested that ABA was superior to special education on a broad range of outcomes (e.g., cognitive functioning, socialization, adaptive behavior) for children with ASD (Ospina et al., 2008). In community practice, several comprehensive treatment programs are characterized as ABA programs or DTT programs. However, the exact number and types of variations of ABA apart from the UCLA training model are not known and have not been well studied (Odom et al., 2010).

A common criticism of the UCLA training model is the tendency to produce overlearned, robotic behaviors in domains that require functional, flexible responses (e.g., language, social skills). While the curriculum teaches specific skills (e.g., vocabulary), it does not teach flexible use of skills to maintain naturalistic social interactions. In addition, although maintenance and generalizability are both theoretically part of the program, generalizability of skills taught has been a particular concern, as the original program was often taught in a single, clinic-type table setting, rather than in real-world settings. Other criticisms of ABA included its use of punishments as well as positive reinforcements (i.e., rewards); revisions of the curriculum included a much heavier emphasis on rewards whenever possible. A continued concern about DTT is feasibility, given its emphasis on high-intensity (up to 40 hr per week) intervention with a one-to-one staffing ratio. Many of these criticisms have been addressed by the neobehavioral and naturalistic approaches described below.

ABA techniques can be used to both increase desired behavior, as well as decrease negative behaviors. In the example below, DTT is used to teach a child the new skill of waving good-bye, the identified target behavior. The antecedent in this example would be the prompt of an individual waving good-bye to the child, after which the child would fail to respond. The goal would be to recreate the situation, then prompt the child to engage in the behavior by modeling the behavior, or by physical prompt or verbal prompt. Using the operant learning technique of shaping, once the individual begins to engage in some aspects of the behavior, for example saying "ba," the therapist engages in the appropriate reinforcement. This type of sequence would be repeated until the target behavior is achieved. Figure 1 outlines this process. See Table 5 for the different techniques that are implemented in ABA.

ABA techniques can be used to both increase desired behavior, as well as decrease negative behaviors

Variations of ABA: Naturalistic Behavior Therapies

Variations of the UCLA training model have emerged in recent years in response to challenges with generalization and spontaneity observed in DTT programs. These programs are often referred to as naturalistic behavior

Table 5
Basic Operant Learning Techniques Used in ABA Programs

Operant learning technique	Description	Example in ABA instruction for people with ASD
Positive reinforcement	Systematic use of positive stimuli (e.g., praise, snack, food, toys) to increase desired behaviors	Tangible reward: preferred food item Social reward: high five
Shaping	Reinforcing approximations of a behavior until target behavior is exhibited	Providing a reward for using "ha" sound when the goal is to say "hi"
Fading	Reducing level of prompting to promote independence	Not using a physical prompt when asking the child to wave
Extinction	Taking away stimuli that maintains a problem behavior	Ignoring screaming hypothesized to be maintained by attention from others
Differential reinforcement	Reinforcing a socially acceptable alternative (e.g., asking for help instead of crying) or absence of a behavior (e.g., 5 min without stereotypy)	The alternative behavior (e.g., using words to express frustration) would be rewarded
Punishment	Applying undesired stimulus (ranging from "no" to physical contact) to reduce problem behaviors	Saying "no"

Note. ABA = applied behavior analysis; ASD = autism spectrum disorder.

therapies and include specific models such as the natural language paradigm (Koegel, O'Dell, & Koegel, 1987), pivotal response treatment (PRT; Koegel, Singh, & Koegel, 2010), and applied verbal behavior model (Sautter & Leblanc, 2006). Naturalistic behavior therapy programs are rooted in the principles of behavior analysis and emphasize generalizing and increasing flexibility of skills. Toward this goal, naturalistic behavior therapies utilize well-validated strategies to promote generalization from the operant conditioning literature, including but not limited to:

1. teaching across multiple settings,
2. using multiple examples/stimuli,
3. transferring skills in more naturalistic (e.g., loosely structured) environments, and
4. using naturalistic reinforcers.

The various forms of naturalistic behavior interventions appear similar in practice but may differ in specific qualities such as treatment modality (e.g., parent/therapist delivery, center-based) and hypothesized mechanism. Most naturalistic approaches emphasize using naturally occurring ("incidental") interactions to promote target goals. Furthermore, these interventions focus on "child choice," maximizing the child's natural motivations, and manipulating the environment to elicit desired behaviors. For example, therapists using naturalistic behavior approaches may place a preferred toy (e.g., bubbles) in a hard-to-reach location and require the child to engage in a specific behavior to access the toy. Similar principles of shaping, fading, chaining, and reinforcement as used in DTT would be used to elicit this response. The child early in instruction may be given the toy when she/he points to it. However, further down the instructional path, the child may be required to point, look at the parent, and say "bubbles please" to receive the toy. In practice, naturalistic approaches are often used in conjunction with DTT to generalize skills taught in one-to-one DTT training sessions.

PRT is a well-known approach with the most empirical support of existing naturalistic behavior programs. PRT emphasizes teaching "pivotal," early-developing social skills thought to serve as the foundation for more generalized social and academic skills. These pivotal skills include social initiation, self-initiation, responding to multiple cues, and self-management. The treatment model is based in the principles of learning theory but uses a child-directed rather than the adult-directed approach of the DTT/UCLA training model. The child-directed teaching sessions may provide a play setting with desired and less-preferred objects arranged in such a way that the child must use eye gaze, pointing, facial expressions, etc. to request unreachable desired objects. PRT may be conducted in the clinic or home, and it often utilizes parents as therapists to reinforce teaching these pivotal social behaviors. While PRT by its definition is not as explicitly curriculum-based as some of the other variants of ABA, a guidebook manual is available by its main authors (Koegel & Koegel, 2006). PRT and modifications of PRT have received some support in the literature, primarily in single-subject case series and open-label studies. While no large-scale controlled study has been conducted to demonstrate the efficacy of PRT as a comprehensive intervention program, studies have demonstrated the efficacy of PRT programming to improve individual skills such as play (Stahmer, 1995).

Skills taught in PRT: Social initiation Self-initiation Responding to multiple cues Self-management

A core component of PRT is the use of motivation to teach skills. Child-preferred stimuli are chosen, and parents are taught to use instruction when the child is attending; once the child responds, parents are encouraged to increase the child's motivation by reinforcement with preferred activities. PRT emphasizes using the child's natural environment to select reinforcers. If the goal is for the child to say a specific word, then the child is reinforced by being given the object, or playing with the object. Another technique used is teaching new skills along with already mastered skills, with the goal of reducing frustration. Finally, in PRT like in other ABA approaches (e.g., DTT), operant conditioning strategies such as shaping and fading are used, and approximations of the desired behavior are reinforced during the learning process (Koegel et al., 2010). A recent variation of PRT is the Nova Scotia early intensive behavioral intervention model, which combines parent training with direct behavioral intervention. No controlled studies have evaluated the Nova Scotia model, but a naturalistic study demonstrated gains in language and decreases in behavior problems after 1 year of intervention (Smith et al., 2010). The same study demonstrated improvement in symptoms of autism in children with IQ > 50.

Verbal behavior analysis is a widely used naturalistic behavior therapy. Verbal behavior treatments adopt B. F. Skinner's theories on language development – in particular, the functions of speech, such as mands (requests) and tacts (labels). The verbal behavior approach, like earlier forms of ABA, relies on a thorough baseline assessment, with comprehensive and systematic data. While there are many publications that are used to implement verbal behavior, the Assessment of Basic Language and Learning Skills – Revised (ABLLS-R; Parrington, 2010) and the Verbal Behavior Milestones Assessment and Placement Program (Sundberg, 2008) are widely used assessment tools and curriculum guides that have also been adopted by schools for goal selection and tracking. To date, no controlled studies have evaluated verbal models of treatment as a comprehensive program, although studies of specific teaching strategies have been published and suggest that several aspects, including mand training, are effective (Bourret, Vollmer, & Rapp, 2004).

> **Verbal behavior treatments emphasizes the functions of speech, such as mands (requests) and tacts (labels)**

Evaluation of effect sizes in EIBI has been limited by several factors including the historical reliance on single-subject experimental designs in the ABA traditions that underlie EIBI approaches and educational, rather than medical, models adopted in most intervention programs. However, several randomized controlled trials (RCTs) have been conducted in recent years, although typically relying on quasirandomized or clinical control trials (e.g., comparison to no-treatment or treatment as usual). A recent review of five studies reported strong reservations related to the risk for bias and reliance on non-RCT designs (Reichow, Barton, Boyd, & Hume, 2012). With these limitations in mind, positive outcomes were reported across measures and were reported using Hedges's g statistic. IQ ($g = .76$), daily communication skills ($g = .74$), and adaptive behavior ($g = .69$) demonstrated the strongest effects, followed by receptive language ($g = .57$), daily living skills ($g = .55$), expressive language ($g = .50$), and socialization ($g = .42$). Case Vignette 3 provides an example of using a DTT intervention for a toddler with ASD.

Case Vignette 3
Discrete Trial Training (ABA) for a Toddler With ASD

Jim is a 3.5-year-old boy who has received applied behavior analysis (ABA) services for the past year. Jim's prenatal, perinatal, and early infant development was relatively unremarkable according to his mother's report and pediatric records. His only significant medical history includes frequent ear infections starting around 8 months of age. According to his mother, Jim's language and social development progressed at an age-appropriate rate until around the age of 13 months. At that time, Jim's parents noticed a marked reduction in his babbling, eye contact, and social interactions. A number of medical evaluations were conducted at this time. The neurological examination and audiological exam concluded that the brain imaging and hearing and behavioral responses were normal, indicating the delays in his communication and social development could not primarily be due to deficits in auditory perception.

Jim received daily instructional services through his local early intervention program. Progress reports indicated he was making improvements in the domains of attentive skills, nonverbal communication, and receptive language but limited progress in speech. He was able to imitate a few isolated consonant sounds (e.g., ba, da, key), but was unable to combine sounds into meaningful words. Jim was also having difficulty with stimulus control as he typically would respond to most instructions with a predictable sequence (e.g., giving "bu," "ya," "wa" to the instruction "what color").

Jim was evaluated for ABA services with an agency specializing in discrete trial training (DTT/ABA). He had difficulty articulating consonant and vowel sounds, and his spontaneous speech was restricted to unprompted imitation of simple words. Socially, he engaged primarily in isolate play, had difficulty sustaining social interactions with his older sister, and rarely initiated social contact. He demonstrated a relative strength in receptive language as he could nonverbally identify numerous colors and objects when provided with verbal labels. It was recommended that Jim receive 20 hr of one-on-one ABA services per week.

Goals were developed across critical areas of development for a young toddler/ preschool-aged child. Target skills were identified in the following domains: speech/language, play, motor skills, social engagement, and behavior. Speech/ language goals targeted increased motor imitation, pointing, and use of picture symbols to communicate preferences (e.g., snack, DVD). Social/play goals targeted increased object imitation with age-appropriate toys (e.g., rolling a car), imitation of peer play, and taking turns with toy play.

Daily and weekly progress monitoring was conducted by direct service providers through daily data collection on each goal, and weekly graphical charting reviewed by the program supervisor. Parent meetings were held on a monthly basis to review progress on each goal and domain, making adjustments as needed depending on the pace of progress or stagnation in each skill.

Operant principles of modeling, shaping, fading, and reinforcement were used to teach new skills. For example, a focus of Jim's social goals was imitation of peer play. Since Jim liked particular toys, therapists started with the goal of teaching Jim to imitate his peers' actions with toys. Using fading techniques, reinforcement was initially provided for imitating actions, with physical prompting from the examiner (e.g., hand-over-hand prompting with verbal prompt – "play with Billy"). As therapy progressed, physical prompting was faded from hand-over-hand, to a physical prompt on the elbow, to a light touch on the shoulder, to the verbal prompt alone. For the language component, modeling desired sounds (e.g., "ball") and shaping were used to teach single-word imitation. Word approximations were reinforced (e.g., "ba" for "ball"). In general, tickles and snack rewards (e.g., Goldfish snack crackers) were powerful reinforcers and were used during this initial therapy period, pairing them with verbal praise and positive affect (e.g., smiling, high-fives).

After approximately 6 months of ABA intervention, Jim had made marked improvements in communication and social skills. He had approximately 20 spoken words that he used on a regular basis, and he was imitating short phrases and sentences. The improvement in verbal communication was accompanied by a noticeable improvement in social skills. He had more spontaneous initiations with adults and had a play repertoire that included symbolic and cooperative play (when prompted). His current program is focused on skills required for successful functioning in preschool environments, such as conversational speech and cooperative play.

After one year of intervention, developmental delays are still evident although to a lesser degree. In the domain of communication, he has reached age-appropriate levels on many expressive and receptive language goals. With the exception of the "f" sound, his articulation skills are at age-level. He continues to have difficulty with pronoun use and with sustaining conversation. Preacademic and concept formation skills are a relative strength, with current goals including number concepts (e.g., "how many"), prepositions, and gender identification. These are skills that are expected for children entering preschool and kindergarten and thus are appropriate targets for future intervention.

Structured Teaching

Structured teaching is a comprehensive treatment model designed specifically for the unique cognitive, behavioral, and learning styles of people with ASD. Structured teaching emphasizes using both environmental supports and instructional strategies that capitalize on the strengths of people with ASD, particularly in the domain of visual processing. Structured teaching was endorsed through an education program funded by the state of North Carolina, specifically designed to support students with ASD, and known as the Division Treatment and Education of Autistic and Related Communication-Handicapped Children (TEACCH) program. The four components of the TEACCH model include providing a structured environment for the individual; harvesting individual strengths, specifically strengths surrounding visual skills, to increase ability in weaker areas; motivating through specific interests; and supporting communication that is initiated by the individual.

While TEACCH is not manualized into one specific curriculum, the general approach capitalizes on the strengths of individuals with ASD in visual processing and visual memory by incorporating visual supports throughout the program. Specific visual support strategies are incorporated into organizing the classroom physical environment (e.g., color coding areas for different activities), daily schedules (e.g., picture or written schedules), and teaching new skills (e.g., in work stations or through visual schedules). Today, visual supports developed with the TEACCH program are considered standard educational practices with young children and children with other developmental needs, and TEACCH methods are well supported in the literature (Mesibov & Shea, 2010). See Figure 2 for an example of a visual daily schedule for a child.

Examining overall outcomes from the TEACCH program, a meta-analysis of 13 studies indicated a pooled effect size of 0.47; lower effect sizes were

> **Components of TEACCH:**
> Providing a structured environment
> Harvesting individual strengths
> Motivating through specific interests
> Supporting initiated communication

Figure 2
Sample individual student schedule used with structured teaching models.

reported for preschool-aged children, 0.29, while larger effect sizes were observed for school-aged children, 0.53, and adults, 0.81. The effect size reported in adults suggests that there is some promise for use of both visual supports and work systems for improving functional outcomes for adults with ASD and intellectual disability living in residential facilities, a group for which few other treatment options are available (Van Bourgondien, Reichle, & Schopler, 2003).

Other Comprehensive Educational Models

TEACCH was among the first ASD-specific interventions, and it provided the precedent for focusing treatment of ASD within educational settings. Other educational programs incorporating various treatment components and philosophies have been developed in recent years. The Learning Experiences: Alternative Programs for Preschoolers and Parents (LEAP) is a program that utilizes ABA approaches using naturalistic teaching strategies in early education classroom settings, with a focus on integrating children with ASD with typically developing children. A recent RCT suggested that children enrolled in LEAP classrooms demonstrated significant gains in language and social skills, and reduced problem behavior over a 2-year period, relative to a comparison group of children whose instructors were given the LEAP manual but no explicit training (Strain & Bovey, 2011).

Another comprehensive program designed to be delivered within educational programs is Social Communication Emotion Regulation Transactional Support (SCERTS). SCERTS integrates strategies from several commonly used approaches including the ABA, TEACCH, and PRT educational frameworks (Prizant, Wetherby, Rubin, & Laurent, 2003). The model focuses on the relationship between communication, emotional development, and emotional regulation, and emphasizes the use of visual support for instruction. A family-centered approach to intervention is utilized, and parents are encouraged to develop age-appropriate treatment goals. SCERTS has not been evaluated as a comprehensive treatment program.

Developmental Models

Relationship-based/developmental models include popular programs such as the developmental, individual-difference, relationship-based/floortime model (also known as the DIR/Floortime or Greenspan model). Comprehensive programs based on Floortime approaches are popular, but to date there have been few studies documenting the success of this program. However, a recently published RCT suggests positive outcomes on measures of unblinded ratings of autism severity and treatment-specific measures of social development milestones relevant to the treatment, which were maintained at a 1-year follow-up (Pajareya & Nopmaneejumruslers, 2011, 2012).

DIR/Floortime teaches parents to start from the level of the child in building relationships

Created by child psychiatrist Stanley Greenspan, the DIR/Floortime model is focused on helping children form strong relationships with caregivers through expanding "circles of communication" and teaching parents to start from the level of the child in building relationships. The intervention emphasizes following the child's lead during play, and outlines several developmental milestones viewed as critical for a child's social, emotional, and cognitive development. These milestones include self-regulation, social interest/motivation, social engagement/intimacy, two-way communication, complex communication, emotional ideas, and emotional thinking.

DIR/Floortime may be used both as a primary intervention, and/or in conjunction with other comprehensive programs described above. As a primary, comprehensive intervention, the intervention typically occurs daily, for several hours, in a one-on-one format with a parent–child or therapist–child dyad. While the model requires evaluation in systematic research studies, aspects of this treatment perspective have influenced other treatment programs. For example, one technique includes imitating a child's actions/behaviors (e.g., copying a child's repetitive hand movements) as one way of opening and closing circles of communication.

The relationship-development intervention (RDI; Gutstein, 2001) is a popular, developmentally based, and parent-directed intervention designed to build social, emotional, and cognitive abilities in children with ASD. The model emphasizes building core, relational skills in contrast to instrumental social behaviors taught in many social skills curricula. The relational skills targeted include, but are not limited to, nonverbal communication (e.g., gestural, emotion, synchrony) and social communication (e.g., humor). RDI outlines eight specific treatment goals hypothesized to facilitate development of contextually appropriate social ability: collaboration, deliberation, flexibility, fluency, friendship, initiative, responsibility, and self-management. Parents work with an RDI consultant to identify a child's level across social domains and are taught to scaffold targeted social domains throughout the daily routine (i.e., guided participation). Parent-delivered treatment in the natural environment is believed to be important in developing flexible and appropriate social abilities, referred to as dynamic intelligence. Current research is fairly limited, with one study conducted by the developers suggesting less severe ASD symptoms as measured by unblinded raters (Gutstein, Burgess, & Montfort, 2007).

Variations of Comprehensive Treatment Programs: Integrative Behavioral-Developmental Models

As mentioned above, developmentally anchored and relationship-based perspectives have been incorporated as adjunctive therapies to ABA interventions as well. The early start Denver model (ESDM) is an integrative model that incorporates ABA principles into a developmental framework. ESDM includes naturalistic ABA procedures with a focus on social, emotional, and relationship development. The treatment targets very young children (often < 3 years) and combines center-based and home-based delivery. Parents are trained to deliver approximately 25 % of treatment sessions within the ESDM model. In an RCT, children received 2 years of 30-hr/week of ESDM treatment or community-as-usual treatment (Dawson et al., 2010). Those receiving ESDM treatment demonstrated greater improvements in ASD symptoms, cognitive functioning, and adaptive skills than those receiving community-based treatment. ESDM has generated substantial enthusiasm by investigators and providers, and has been disseminated widely. While replications are in progress, a published report on parent-delivered ESDM (i.e., services provided without a clinic or direct therapist intervention component) suggests parent-only delivery was not sufficient in producing outcomes matching those in the more intensive, comprehensive intervention, and was not substantially different from a community-based

ESDM is an integrative model that incorporates ABA principles into a developmental framework

intervention comparison. Results suggest intensity of intervention may be as important as type and quality of intervention (Rogers et al., 2012).

4.1.5   Targeted Psychosocial Treatment Programs for Social Communication Impairments

Impairments in socialization are the central, unifying feature in ASD. While certain social impairments are unique to ASD, social deficits in general are linked to debilitating functional impairments across psychiatric conditions (Denham et al., 2003). In typically developing children, strong social skills and peer acceptance are among the most positive prognostic indicators of academic achievement and mental health. Unfortunately, the most effective early intervention approaches for children with ASD have not been shown to have the same positive impact on social impairments as seen in other domains such as speech/language and intellectual disability.

Treatments for socialization impairments in ASD are built on a strong body of research on how social processes depart from "typical" development. Studies of early-developing social behaviors in infants and toddlers highlight impairments in early-appearing social skills believed to serve as the "social glue" for infants and babies to learn about their world, regulate emotions, and navigate relationships. These early-developing social behaviors include imitation, gesturing, eye gaze, emotional expression, and shared attention (e.g., joint attention).

Individuals with ASD without intellectual disability also have substantial socialization deficits, particularly in discerning the subtleties of complex social interactions. For example, these individuals can often identify basic emotions, but research on visual scanning patterns in social situations suggests these individuals may use alternative strategies that may not be sufficient when social requirements are more complex and dynamic (Pelphrey et al., 2002). Similarly, while children with ASD without intellectual disability may pass basic ToM (i.e., they understand the perspectives/intentions of others), they continue to have difficulty understanding the intent behind nonliteral speech (Martin & McDonald, 2004).

Treatments in older children and individuals are complicated by the compounding impact of social disability across time, particularly as it relates to chronic social isolation, associated mental health concerns, and chronic underemployment/unemployment. For example, individuals with ASD and comorbid ADHD may be at greater risk for peer rejection and significant social dysfunction than individuals with ASD or ADHD alone (Montes & Halterman, 2007). The relatively recent focus on issues facing older children, adolescents, and adults with ASD has limited the empirical evidence to guide practice in the treatment of higher level core deficits.

Targeted Socialization Treatments for Young Children With ASD
Treatments for socialization impairments in young children with ASD typically focus on improving specific skills deficits as well as improving interactions/engagement with adults and peers. Commonly used models are described below and include behavioral skills training, social scripts, video modeling, and social stories.

Behavioral skills training (BST) refers to a class of treatments that utilize principles of behavioral analysis and social learning to teach target skills. BST is an approach that can be applied to a range of skills deficits in children with and without disabilities such as compliance (e.g., following group instructions), safety skills (e.g., stranger-danger), as well as social skills. BST programs incorporate instruction, modeling, rehearsal, and feedback to teach target behaviors and are delivered in a range of settings and by a range of providers.

**Using BST to teach basic social skills:
Joint attention
Symbolic play
Social initiation
Greetings**

BST has been evaluated primarily in single-subject case design research, and has been applied to a range of social skills including eye contact, play skills (e.g., object imitation, symbolic play), social initiation, sustaining interactions, greetings, and sustaining interactions with peers (Kasari & Patterson, 2012). BST may also be used to promote generalization of existing skills in appropriate environments and/or individuals (e.g., peers vs. adults). BST for joint attention training may break down shared attention into specific behavioral components including using eye contact, gesture, and speech to engage in basic aspects of shared attention (e.g., pointing to share interest) as well as more complex shared attention behaviors (e.g., pointing, showing, and checking to ensure engagement of peer/adult). Research on a particular form of joint attention training referred to as joint attention symbolic play engagement and regulation (JASPER) suggests that joint attention training has the potential to facilitate both joint attention, as well as symbolic play, and thus serves as a foundation for learning more advanced social behaviors (Kasari, Paparella, Freeman, & Jahromi, 2008).

Another promising behavioral method for enhancing social skills in young children with ASD is referred to as reciprocal imitation training (RIT). RIT is a variation of PRT, based on research highlighting the importance of imitation as a foundational social and cognitive skill (Ingersoll & Schreibman, 2006). RIT promotes reciprocal imitation through therapist imitation of child behavior and vocalizations (Klinger & Dawson, 1992) and "linguistic mapping," in which the therapist describes the action the pair is engaged in (e.g., "we are making duck sounds"). In addition, naturalistic behavior strategies are incorporated to promote learning (e.g., prompting, use of natural reinforcers, including motivating objects, promoting child choice). RIT improves both imitation and pretend play in young children with ASD, with skills generalizing to untrained situations (e.g., new therapists, materials). Other critical social skills improved after RIT, including joint attention and spontaneous play (Ingersoll & Schreibman, 2006).

Treatments for School-Aged and Older Individuals With ASD

Social skills training (SST) is a commonly used strategy for addressing socialization deficits in verbal children

Social skills training (SST) is a commonly used strategy for addressing socialization deficits in verbal children with ASD. SST may take the form of individual or group therapy, is applied to younger and older individuals, and may address a range of deficits. Most SST programs occur within the context of social skills groups, and as such the focus on this section will apply primarily to data from social skills groups. However, it should be acknowledged that most curricula used within social skills groups in practice have been applied in both individual and group formats, and it is unclear what constitutes an optimal approach (see Table 6).

Table 6
Summary of Social Skills Training Approaches

Treatment	Target developmental level / age group	Treatment delivery	Social skills taught using the approach	Description of treatment
Behavioral skills training	All ages	Therapists All settings (school, clinic, home) Individual, group	Various: e.g., eye contact, sharing, joining in groups, turn taking	Instruction, modeling, rehearsal, and feedback are used to teach target skills in structured settings
Naturalistic behavior therapies (e.g., pivotal response training)	Preschool, early school age	Therapists, parents Clinic, home Individual	Imitation, social motivation, self-management, self-initiation	Uses a child-directed approach, ABA strategies, and natural reinforcers to build foundational (i.e., pivotal) social behaviors
Peer training	School age	Therapists, peers School, clinic Individual	Social interactions with typically developing peers	Peers taught to engage children with ASD; offer social support; initiating play
Video modeling	Preschool, middle school	Therapists (models), child (learner) School, home Individual	Social skills, communication skills, play skills	Target behavior is modeled, or learner engages in target behavior, and video is viewed at later time
Social stories	Preschool, middle school	Therapists All settings Individual	Social skills, behavioral problems, communication skills	Provides detailed description of social situations and appropriate responses

Table 6 (continued)

Treatment	Target developmental level / age group	Treatment delivery	Social skills taught using the approach	Description of treatment
Cognitive behavior therapy models	School age, adults	Therapist Clinic, home Individual, group	Social skills, anxiety problems	Uses behavioral techniques to decrease anxiety symptoms, improve social skills
Relationship-based models	Preschool, early school age	Therapists, caregiver Clinic, home Individual	Social motivation, social engagement, self-regulation	Developmental approach – following the child's leads during play

Note. ABA = applied behavior analysis; ASD = autism spectrum disorder.

Social skills groups typically enroll school-aged children (2–8 children/group) and are delivered in clinics and schools on a weekly basis for 12 or more weeks. A meta-analysis of five studies of social skills groups for children and adolescents indicated a mean effect size of 0.47 for improved social competence, which was measured differently across studies, and a mean effect size of 0.41 for improved quality of life (Reichow, Steiner, & Volkmar, 2012).

Several methodological challenges remain in evaluating the efficacy of social skills interventions. Critical issues include the limited availability of RCTs employing active treatment comparators, and limited data on the generalization and maintenance of treatment effects. While several curricula have been developed, treatment targets range from teaching discrete, instrumental social behaviors (e.g., joining in a group, offering help, making social phone calls), to more ASD-specific impairments in social cognition (e.g., emotion recognition, ToM) (DeRosier et al., 2011; Frankel et al., 2010; Gantman, Kapp, Orenski, & Laugeson, 2012).

Meta-analytic reports and reviews present an overall mixed picture of treatment efficacy (White, Keonig, & Scahill, 2007). However, a few recent reviews suggest the treatment modality as a whole appears to produce positive outcomes in school-aged children. Programs evaluated in the literature tend to be structured, manual-based, curricula-driven skills training groups; they appear to produce greatest effects on parent ratings of social competence, and have relative weak to minimal influence on cognitive and functional outcomes.

Published, commercially available social skills manuals include several with some empirical support, including PEERS (Laugeson et al., 2012), social skills group intervention (S.S.GRIN; DeRosier et al., 2010), and children's friendship training (Frankel et al., 2010). While social skills curricula differ in age groups and targets, the general approach is as follows: Individuals are identified within a specified age range, staff are trained in a manualized treatment, ASD, and treatment targets are selected. Depending on the model and program, groups may provide explicit activities to promote generalization (e.g., involving parents or teachers), reinforcement systems, and/or unaffected peer models to facilitate training goals. In the community, social skills groups may also be conducted using play-based, dynamic, as well as recreational models (e.g., focused on special interests, video games). These last models have less evidence for their support in the extant literature.

Other Targeted Treatments Promoting Social Skills Development

Social stories – developing story scripts to help children understand social situations – are a widely used approach for teaching a variety of social skills (Gray, 1998). Given the prerequisite skills required for attending to and comprehending written stories, social stories are typically used with school-aged and older children. Social stories are designed to be nondirective, descriptive stories that are tailored to a child's social skills and behavioral and motivational profile. The developer of the intervention has outlined a prescriptive format for designing social stories that includes a description of what people do, why they do it, and common responses to a social situation. Directive statements are explicitly avoided in the original structure of social stories, although they may be used more often in practice and have been shown to improve the effectiveness of stories. Social stories are believed to provide a framework for

Social stories are nondirective, descriptive stories tailored to a child's social skills and behavioral and motivational profile

understanding and feeling more comfortable in social situations that may not be easily deciphered by individuals with ASD.

Social stories have yet to be evaluated in large-scale well-controlled trials. However, existing research suggests that social stories may be more effective in reducing problem behaviors rather than increasing use of socially appropriate behaviors (Kokina & Kern, 2010). Several factors influence the success of social stories, including verbal comprehension, reading level, and use of directive statements. While data on social story efficacy have been mixed, the most recent and largest RCT suggests that directive statements, when used to promote play skills and administered immediately prior to a play session, are a critical element (Quirmbach, Lincoln, Feinberg-Gizzo, Ingersoll, & Andrews, 2009).

Video modeling is another social skills strategy that can be applied to teaching appropriate social behaviors. Video modeling involves teaching skills using recordings to provide a dynamic visual model and prompts in a video. Similarly to picture schedules, video modeling capitalizes on visual processing abilities in individuals with ASD. Video modeling procedures may include taking videos of the peer or adult models, having the individual with ASD engage in target behaviors (e.g., self-modeling), and/or taking the video from the point of view of the learner. Several single-subject case design studies have been published supporting the effectiveness of variations of video modeling in teaching and in generalizing social skills such as complex play, conversation, and compliments (e.g., Apple, Billingsley, Schwartz, & Carr, 2005).

In addition to direct instruction, social skills treatments have also facilitated skill learning and performance through training peers. Known as peer-mediated intervention (PMI), this approach typically involves developing peers who are coached to interact with people with ASD in a method that facilitates learning new skills and using these skills in environments where children will need them the most. PMIs have been effectively used to facilitate language and social skills, as well as friendship/social networks in preschool- and school-aged children with ASD (Kasari & Patterson, 2012).

4.1.6   Targeted Psychosocial Treatment Programs for Restricted, Repetitive Behaviors and Interests

RRBs are a core feature of ASD and have been found to be among the earliest and most persistent diagnostic markers in the condition (Richler et al., 2010). RRBs include subclasses of behaviors that are presumed to serve different functions. While few treatments are available for the different classes of RRBs, available psychosocial approaches addressing each of these different classes are described here.

ABA strategies for RRBs: Differential reinforcement of alternative behaviors Extinction Response interruption

Behavioral treatments for RRBs have largely focused on reducing repetitive motor behaviors (RMBs) using operant learning (i.e., ABA) strategies such as differential reinforcement of alternative behaviors, extinction, and response interruption. These strategies have been found to be most effective in treating repetitive self-injury, stereotypy, and repetitive object play (Patterson, Smith, & Jelen, 2010). Differential reinforcement of alternative behavior may shape a child to limit hand flapping to leisure or down-time, through simultaneously shaping the behavior of keeping hands in pockets (or on visual prompt of hands on a desk) during work time, while providing opportunities to engage in arousal-regulating motor mannerisms during break periods. Full extinction of motor mannerisms may be undertaken by behavior modification programs but may not be recommended in lieu of strongly developed alternative responses to display frustration, anxiety, and other arousal states related to the original function of the maladaptive behavior. As indicated below, psychopharmacological approaches have also been specifically tested for targeting RRBs.

Interventions for problems related to insistence on sameness or circumscribed interests are less well studied. There is some suggestion that improving engagement in a range of activities (e.g., through using picture activity schedules) and overall independence can improve rigidity and intense preoccupations, but this remains an area requiring further investigation.

4.1.7 Targeted Psychosocial Treatment Programs for Speech/ Language and Other Communication Impairments

Communication-Focused Intervention

Core communication deficits in ASD have more recently been understood to be specific to the social functions of speech/language. The disruption of early social processes in ASD may influence basic elements of speech development. For example, limited social motivation in early childhood likely reduces attention to, and modeling of, human speech that may result in delays in acquiring even basic functional communication skills.

The heterogeneity in speech and communication problems dictates the involvement of a range of professionals in assessment and treatment. Receptive and expressive speech delays are often the purview of educational programs described in prior sections (e.g., DTT), as well as ancillary services such as those provided by speech language pathologists (SLPs). In cases where children present with oral-motor coordination problems, SLPs specializing in apraxia and related conditions may provide tailored interventions like those described below. Treatments for subtle impairments in speech quality (e.g., prosody) and other pragmatic language deficits are not well studied, but may occur as a result of behavioral health treatments such as social skills groups and/or in speech therapy programs. Language interventions embedded within comprehensive programs are described in prior sections, with the following sections focused on commonly used and empirically evaluated *targeted* communication interventions.

Augmentative and Alternative Communication Strategies

Augmentative and alternative communication (AAC) is a commonly used treatment option for minimally verbal individuals with ASD. AAC strategies are viewed as stepping stones to speech development/production, through facilitating the motivation to communicate as well as reducing frustration and behavior problems (see Functional Communication Training, below).

Augmentative and alternative communication (AAC) is used for minimally verbal individuals with ASD

Commonly used AAC strategies include sign language, augmentative communication devices, and picture-based communication systems. While simple signs are often taught to young children who have not yet developed speech, and minimally verbal older children/adults, few individuals with ASD become fluent in sign language (Goldstein, 2002). Many individuals may use modified signs to facilitate basic communication and functional needs (e.g., help, break, bathroom). Some evidence supports the use of "total communication training," a method of combining speech and signs together, to promote receptive and expressive language learning (Yoder & Layton, 1988), particularly in children with limited imitation skills. However these studies did not evaluate the effects of total communication training on facilitating spontaneous use of signs to communicate.

Visually based AAC strategies are widely used with minimally verbal children with ASD. These visually based strategies (see Figure 3) may be incorporated into a systematic instructional program such as the Picture Exchange Communication System® (PECS®) or be used with specialized devices and/or tablet computers. Devices and tablet programs vary in the level of communication facilitated approaches, from showing a simple array of preferred items for requesting, to more sophisticated communication programs that allows construction of full sentences. While most visually based AAC strategies use pictures/symbols, others use typing and/or text-to-speech programming. Tablet use for visually based communication programs in particular is gaining popularity because tablets are more accessible than voice-output communication aides that produce digital speech when the user presses a picture. In a recent meta-analysis, Ganz and colleagues (Ganz, Earles-Vollrath, et al., 2012) found that interventions using devices are effective in improving communication skills, and to a lesser extent social skills and behaviors.

PECS is one widely used and studied instructional program that provides a systematic method for teaching children with ASD to communicate using picture symbols (Bondy & Frost, 1998). It is designed to teach functional communication using the principles of ABA. By beginning with visual symbols, PECS capitalizes on visual processing abilities and hypothesizes that the motivation to communicate will serve as a platform for learning speech. PECS outlines a detailed, six-phase training protocol. Research has shown speech acquisition following PECS training. In practice, picture communication is often taught in the absence of the systematic PECS protocol outlined above. The implementation and integrity of PECS may be an important variable in evaluating success or failure of this intervention in educational and clinical settings.

Instructional strategies are based on principles of operant learning, including stimulus discrimination between visual symbols, shaping communicative response (e.g., handing the teacher a desired symbol), and reinforcement for desired responses. The initial stages of PECS involve two teachers, one to prompt the child to hand a picture symbol to an adult and the other to serve as the communication partner. As the program progresses, the child is taught to seek a desired picture from a selection, and to bring that picture to an adult. The next step (see Figure 3) would include a verb-noun combination (I want book). Some children eventually progress to constructing full sentences with picture symbols.

Two recent meta-analyses analyzed data from 13 group design studies (Ganz, Davis, Lund, Goodwyn, & Simpson, 2012) and 24 single-subject design studies (Ganz, Earles-Vollrath, et al., 2012) determined that PECS improved communication skills and had smaller but positive effects on other

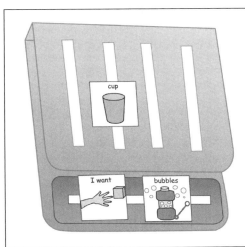

Figure 3.
Sample Picture Exchange Communication System (PECS) board.
When a learner wants a desired item (e.g., cup or bubbles), the learner will
go to their communication book, place the 'I want' card and the 'bubbles'
card on a sentence strip, take the sentence strip off the book, and hand it to a
communicative partner.
Image provided with permission by Pyramid Educational Consultants, Inc.
(http://www.pecs.com). All rights reserved.

behaviors. In addition, studies have demonstrated the benefit of PECS in promoting speech acquisition, with improvements seen in spontaneous communication, imitated speech, and mean length of utterance (Howlin, Gordon, Pasco, Wade, & Charman, 2007).

Targeted Treatments for Oral-Motor Impairments in ASD

As previously indicated, ASD may be associated with a range of motor impairments. Prompts for restructuring oral muscular phonetic targets (PROMPT) is a targeted treatment for oral-motor impairments in ASD, adapted from treatment for adults with neurological disorders. PROMPT is believed to integrate sensory, motor, and social domains to promote articulation, speech sound production, and social communication. In the PROMPT approach, a speech therapist uses modeling and physical manipulation of the lips, tongue, and jaw to help the individual learn to form speech sounds in the context of a motivating play session (Rogers et al., 2006). Studies in children with developmental speech disorders, including ASD, are limited at this time.

4.1.8   Behavioral Interventions for Comorbid and Associated Conditions

Recent reviews of behavioral interventions in ASD suggest a fairly limited pool of research-guided evidence-based practices for ASD-associated symptoms. Several promising programs have been adapted from the treatments of other psychiatric conditions, including adaptations of parent management training

(PMT) for disruptive behavior disorders and cognitive behavior therapy (CBT) for anxiety disorders. In addition, behavioral interventions for comorbid medical conditions, particularly sleep disturbance and food selectivity, have been developed for people with ASD and will also be detailed in this section.

Disruptive Behaviors

Psychosocial interventions for disruptive behavior disorders in people with ASD have their roots in the fields of behavioral analysis and positive behavior support. These models emphasize the importance of directly observing behaviors, a focus on function rather than topography, and linking assessment with intervention through consistent, systematic data collection. FBAs form the foundation of psychosocial approaches to addressing problem behaviors across conditions. FBAs are mandated in the United States by the Individuals With Disabilities Education Act (IDEA; Individuals With Disabilities Education Act of 2004) for use in the treatment of problem behaviors in students with disabilities, and are a central component of the positive behavioral support movement.

Functions of Problem Behaviors:
Escaping demands
Social attention
Obtaining reward
Self-directed motivation

Using the assumption that all behavior is learned and maintained through the environment, implementation of an FBA may involve having the therapist (the behavioral analyst) essentially conduct "experiments" that vary elements of the environment to isolate the antecedents and consequences that are maintaining the behavior. Data are collected within each "condition," and hypotheses are developed regarding the functions of each behavior.

Common functions for problem behaviors in children include escape from demands, social attention, obtaining a tangible reward, and/or self-stimulatory/self-directed motivations. In situations when direct manipulation of problem behaviors may not be feasible, "descriptive FBAs" may be conducted in which structured observations are used to take data from the natural environment (e.g., school) to gain understanding of situations that elicit undesired behaviors and those that do not. Direct observations of behavior across multiple settings are a fundamental component of FBAs, and must be used in both assessing and treating problem behavior in this model.

Figure 4 provides a depiction of the components and outcomes from an FBA. Systematic data collection via direct observations of a child in multiple settings suggested that the behavior occurred across multiple periods of the school day, and was related to deficits in communication – with the specific antecedent being the inability to communicate the need for more understanding of transitions. The proposed intervention was designed with prevention as a primary goal, ideally through teaching attention and use of a picture activity schedule to reduce anxiety about upcoming transitions. In addition, the child was taught to use a "break card" which was a visual cue that was handed to teachers when he became overwhelmed and needed to find a quiet place to recalibrate. FBAs inherently link assessment to treatment, and create a dynamic, iterative process by which procedures and interventions are refined until effective treatments for target skills are found.

In studies, the experimental functional analyses described above are used to establish the function of the problem behaviors (Durand & Carr, 1991). The time-consuming and costly nature of conducting experimental functional assessments has resulted in the development of brief descriptive methods.

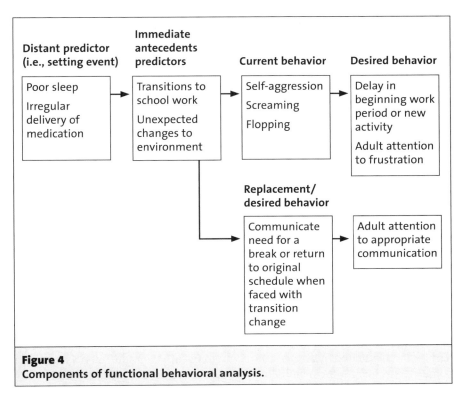

Figure 4
Components of functional behavioral analysis.

These brief functional assessments may include paper-pencil report forms, brief interviews, and/or direct observations without experimental manipulations. The literature on the utility of the indirect methods of functional assessment is mixed, with some research indicating a strong correlation between descriptive and experimental analyses, and other research indicating that descriptive assessments produce less-clear and less-specific results.

Functional Communication Training

Functional communication training (FCT) refers to a differential reinforcement procedure in which maladaptive behaviors are replaced by alternative, communicative behaviors (Durand & Carr, 1991). The premise of FCT is that "problem behavior is communication" and improved communication can provide language-impaired individuals with a socially appropriate, *functionally equivalent* response to maladaptive behavior. FBA is inherent to FCT. For example, many individuals with ASD struggle to ask for help in times of need. In lieu of this basic communication strategy, individuals may resort to using maladaptive behaviors such as self-stimulatory behaviors or aggressive behaviors. FCT would use FBA to assess the function of problem behaviors as reflecting a need either for attention or to escape from demand, and subsequently provide developmentally appropriate methods to ask for help (e.g., teach the child to use a visual symbol for help).

The premise of functional communication training (FCT) is that "problem behavior is communication"

Parent Management Training

Widely used and efficacious in the treatment of children with disruptive behavior disorders, PMT has been applied to the treatment of problem behaviors in children with ASD (Chronis, Jones, & Raggi, 2006). PMT is also rooted in the operant conditioning literature, and as such shares a theoretical platform with positive behavior support strategies. However, PMT is different in its focus on empowering parents through education and instruction to implement effective behavior management strategies in the home. In individuals with ASD, PMT may be delivered in individual parent-coaching sessions and/or workshop/group formats. In practice, several of the early intervention and comprehensive programs incorporate behavior management strategies into the parent-training components of their treatments.

Results from RCTs support the use of PMT as an EST in ASD (Aman et al., 2009; Sofronoff, Leslie, & Brown, 2004). The composition of PMT treatment packages vary considerably and often incorporate elements tailored to the specific needs of people with ASD. Sofronoff, Leslie, and Brown (2004) randomized parents of children with Asperger's disorder to PMT workshops, individual PMT, or wait-list control groups. Results indicated parents in both PMT groups reported their children exhibited fewer and less intense problems. The manualized program incorporated social skills instruction such as comic strip conversations and social stories with traditional PMT strategies such as planned ignoring and token economies.

Anxiety Disorders

The poor distinction between core symptoms of ASD and anxiety provide some constraints for the development and advancement of effective treatments for anxiety disorders in ASD. The vast majority of research on anxiety in ASD has been conducted with verbal children. Future research on the relationship between core symptoms, arousal dysregulation, and anxiety subtypes (e.g., separation, specific phobia, OCD) will be necessary to help guide treatments for the full spectrum of individuals with ASD who are managing anxiety-related symptoms in daily life.

Several treatment approaches address these challenges by providing comprehensive, modular treatment packages that can be individually tailored to the presentation of the child (Wood et al., 2009). The two core components of CBT programs for treating anxiety in children with ASD represent essential ingredients of all CBT-based anxiety treatments: teaching anxiety coping skills and applying/practicing strategies. Most packages include traditional CBT treatment components such as self-monitoring, emotion recognition, relaxation, exposure and response prevention, cognitive restructuring, and in vivo skills practice. ASD-specific adaptations typically involve incorporation of social skills instruction (e.g., emotion recognition, social stories) and visual supports. Increased parent involvement is another important adaptation to traditional CBT interventions. The sample subjective units of distress scale (SUDS) and coping chart (see Figure 5) exemplifies ASD-tailored strategies to manage executive control problems. This SUDS incorporates a visual prompt for the SUDS rating on the coping list, including sensory-related and interest-related options on the coping list, and use of visual supports.

A 2013 meta-analysis of CBT interventions for anxiety symptoms in ASD provides some insight into the overall effect of available treatments described (Sukhodolsky, Bloch, Panza, & Reichow, 2013). Eight studies were included in the meta-analysis, and seven out of eight of those studies used wait-list or treat-

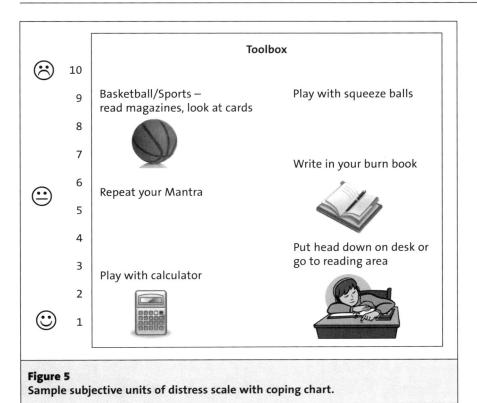

Figure 5
Sample subjective units of distress scale with coping chart.

ment-as-usual controls. Changes in clinician and parent-report measures of anxiety symptoms suggest overall large effect sizes with Cohen's *d* statistics ranging from 1.19 (clinician ratings) to 1.21 (parent ratings). However, these studies require further evaluation against attention controls to evaluate the specificity of treatment effects for CBT compared with less specific treatment approaches.

4.1.9 Psychopharmacological Treatments for Core and Associated Conditions

Psychopharmacological treatments are increasingly used in the clinical care of individuals with ASD, and this increase is documented by the sharp rise in prescription patterns over the past 10 years (Aman, Lam, & Van Bourgondien, 2005). When considering all pharmacological treatments, including psychotropic medications, medications for associated medical conditions (e.g., sleep), and CAM approaches, surveys suggest approximately 50–75 % of individuals with ASD are taking one or more medications. When considering psychotropic medication alone, polypharmacy is used in approximately one third of children with ASD, with higher rates (60–80 %) observed in adolescents and adults (Aman et al., 2005; Coury et al., 2012; Esbensen, Greenberg, Seltzer, & Aman, 2009). Increased reliance on medications may be attributed to several variables, including increased recognition of co-occurring psychiatric disorders in individuals with ASD, with and without comorbid intellectual disability (Tsiouris, Kim, Brown, Pettinger, & Cohen, 2013). However, as

Few psychotropic medications have shown effectiveness in addressing core ASD impairments

reviewed below, with the exception of high-risk treatments such as atypical antipsychotic use in treating irritability/aggression, few psychotropic medications have been shown to be effective in addressing core ASD or associated impairments, or modifying developmental trajectories.

In clinical practice, the pharmacological care of children with ASD is ideally conducted by clinicians with experience in treating children with developmental disabilities. Few treatments are specifically indicated for core or associated symptoms of ASD, and some of those that are specifically indicated have risky side effects. In addition, even experienced physicians report several challenges in translating pharmacological models for treatment of similar symptoms in other pediatric conditions to individuals with ASD. Challenges include increased sensitivity to side effects including hyperactivity and irritability, as well as atypical responses to medications.

Initially, the approach to identifying promising medications for people with ASD drew on careful clinical observations of similar phenotypes in other psychiatric and developmental disorders, as well as trial-and-error treatments during a time when limited data were available to inform practice. Early studies adopted treatments for disorders with similar topography and symptom domains such as use of atypical antipsychotics for irritability/aggression in schizophrenia, stimulants for inattention and hyperactivity in ADHD, and selective serotonin reuptake inhibitors in treatment of repetitive/rigid behaviors in OCD. The symptom-based approach led to a few promising treatments, particularly in the domain of treatments for irritability/aggression. The earlier approaches also stimulated back-translation of clinical findings to identify potential pathophysiological substrates of core and associated symptoms in ASD (e.g., serotonin dysregulation).

Pharmacological Interventions for Core Symptoms

The core symptoms of ASD include uniquely developmentally based social communication skills deficits, similar to the "negative" symptoms of other disorders, suggesting that they represent impairment based on the lack of developmentally appropriate skills. Given the distinctiveness of these types of deficits with respect to other symptoms that are the target of psychopharmacological treatments (e.g., depression, anxiety, psychosis), negative symptoms have long been considered notoriously difficult to treat. Some have argued that psychopharmacological treatment for these symptoms and related intellectual disability may not be possible through a direct route, but it is more likely that such medications could only work through mechanisms such as plasticity and changes to synapse morphology – basically expediting a learning process that will need to occur through educational/behavioral interventions (Castrén, Elgersma, Maffei, & Hagerman, 2012).

In light of this complexity, very few psychopharmacological agents have been tested specifically to target the social communication deficit domain in ASD. However, more recently a few nontraditional agents that may be considered psychopharmacological in nature are being tried. For instance, oxytocin, a neuropeptide long thought to be involved in maternal bonding and affiliative behaviors, is now being tested directly for improvements in social communication.

While social communication deficits may be considered as negative symptoms, RRBs can be considered positive symptoms, and they overlap conceptually with symptoms of disorders such as OCD, a disorder that can be effectively treated with medication. Several medications, including those used for OCD and other anxiety disorders in children, have been tested in targeting RRBs. Selective serotonin reuptake inhibitors, including fluoxetine, fluvoxamine, and citalopram, have all undergone RCTs with such aims. While results are weak for efficacy in children, some support for some of the selective serotonin reuptake inhibitors has been found for adults (Farmer, Thurm, & Grant, 2013).

Moreover, a few recent studies that have targeted comorbid psychiatric symptoms have given hints that medications aimed at treating specific associated symptoms such as irritability and aggression may also have a potential impact on the core social communication deficits of ASD. While it is difficult to show whether improvements seen in measures such as adaptive functioning are downstream effects of improvement in the targeted symptom (e.g., irritability), and measurement of effect is difficult when these assessments are not the primary outcome in a treatment study, these results are nonetheless intriguing and warrant further attention.

Pharmacological Interventions for Comorbid Psychiatric Symptoms

Psychiatric comorbidities associated with ASD create substantial burdens on families and society through increased need for services across settings and need for the involvement of multiple care systems/providers. In contrast to cognitive/language impairments where behavioral interventions are a mainstay of treatment, approximately 80 % of children with comorbid mental health conditions were found to be to be treated with at least one medication (see Coury et al., 2012). Pharmacological approaches have been used to address the range of comorbid psychiatric symptoms presenting in people with ASD, including irritability/aggression, self-injury, inattention, and hyperactivity. Few studies are available to inform pharmacological treatment of comorbid anxiety and mood disturbance in ASD, despite common use of antianxiety agents and mood stabilizers in clinical practice (Coury et al., 2012).

Approximately 80% of children with comorbid mental health conditions were treated with at least 1 medication

Atypical Antipsychotics for Irritability/Aggression

Antipsychotics are among the most widely studied pharmacological treatments for people with ASD. Ideally, antipsychotics are considered in conjunction with or following behavioral interventions such as FBA and/or PMT. However, atypical antipsychotics have been increasingly used in recent years, likely associated with FDA-approval of two atypical antipsychotics for the treatment of irritability in children with ASD (risperidone in 2006, aripiprazole in 2009).

Conventional antipsychotics including haloperidol were studied in the 1980s and found to reduce symptoms of irritability and aggression, as well as RRBs. Side effects included sedation and dyskinesias, although the latter were rarely observed in published short-term treatment trials available at that time (Doyle & McDougle, 2012). Atypical antipsychotics, which have properties thought to lower the risk of extrapyramidal symptoms became increasingly used and evaluated as a potential treatment for the associated symptoms of ASD. Published trials of atypical antipsychotics including risperidone (McCracken et al., 2002) and aripiprazole (Marcus et al., 2009) provided support for the efficacy of atypical antipsychotics in treating irritability and aggression in children with ASD. An additional RCT supported efficacy of risperidone in treating irritability/aggression in adults with ASD as well (McDougle et al., 1998). In addition, secondary analyses also suggested improvements in core symptoms such as improved socialization and reduced RRBs. It is unclear whether changes in core symptoms were related to direct actions of atypicals (e.g., via serotonin or glutamate systems) or associated with overall reductions in irritability and arousal facilitating increased engagement and appropriate behavior.

However, the side effect profile of atypical antipsychotics is significant; the most common and most troubling side effects are endocrine and metabolic problems. Studies have reported rapid weight gain (e.g., 25 % increase in body mass indices), Type 2 diabetes, hypertension, as well as aggression/irritability related to food seeking/hunger (Politte & McDougle, 2013). Long-term studies of chronic dosing are needed before one can confidently endorse the long-term, daily, chronic dosing commonly used in clinical practice.

Stimulants and Alpha-Agonists for ADHD in ASD

Clinicians have long recognized the functional impairments caused by symptoms of impulsivity, inattention, and hyperactivity in children with ASD. Treatment of ADHD symptoms in ASD requires careful diagnosis with consideration of how behavioral presentations relate to core deficits (e.g., circumscribed interests, stereotypies) and related medical conditions (e.g., sleep disturbance). Behavioral interventions are recommended as a first-line intervention, and may include previously described approaches such as environmental structure, picture cues, and behavioral assessment/behavior management.

Approximately 49% of children with ASD showed decreased ADHD symptoms profiles on stimulants

The most commonly studied and used psychotropic medications for ADHD symptoms in ASD are stimulants (e.g., methylphenidate and dextroamphetamine). The efficacy of stimulants in treating comorbid ADHD in children with ASD is less dramatic than in ADHD alone, with approximately 49 % of children with ASD showing decreased ADHD symptom profiles compared with 69 % in the large-scale ADHD-only trials (Posey et al., 2007). Treatment with stimulants resulted in reductions in impulsivity, hyperactivity, disinhibition, and inattention (Nickels et al., 2008). Commonly reported side effects include sleep disturbance, appetite changes, headaches, diarrhea, anxiety, and depression.

Guanfacine and clonidine, both alpha-adrenergic agonists, have been used both as adjunctive treatments and as monotherapies in the treatment of ADHD in ASD (Siegel & Beaulieu, 2012). Alpha-agonists are effective as an adjunctive treatment in children with ADHD (without ASD), with data supporting improvements in impulsivity, oppositional behavior, tics, and at times sleep patterns (Mahajan et al., 2012). Studies supporting the widespread use of alpha-agonists for ADHD symptoms in ASD are limited to open-label trials and small RCTs; further investigation is needed to support the application of this practice to children with ASD.

Estimating effect sizes for the various psychopharmacological approaches used to treat associated symptoms of ASD is difficult for several reasons. One particular issue is the relatively high placebo response (30–40 %) observed in several trials. Studies of antipsychotics, particularly risperidone, are among the only agents reporting effect sizes > 0.4 (Siegel & Beaulieu, 2012). In their RCT of methylphenidate, the RUPP Autism Network reported effect sizes of 0.20 to 0.50 (small to medium range) for the ABC Hyperactivity subscale, which is a smaller response rate than that reported in trials of children with ADHD (Research Units on Pediatric Psychopharmacology Autism Network, 2005). Unfortunately, positive, large-scale RCTs are not yet available for the other pharmacological approaches described in this section. Estimation and evaluation of effect sizes and improved treatments are expected in the near future as the field moves toward more targeted treatments which will help reduce heterogeneity in study populations and identify subgroups of individuals for whom treatments may be more effective (Siegel & Beaulieu, 2012). See Case Vignette 4 for an example of a case in which comorbid ADHD ist diagnosed.

Case Vignette 4
Diagnosis and Treatment of Comorbid ADHD

Mark is a 10-year-old boy diagnosed with ASD at age 3. His parents were concerned about his academic functioning and aggressive behaviors. Mark's parents reported that he had always had good grades at school, but since he had started the third grade, his academic performance had been poor. Mark has had some incidents of aggressive behavior at school, pushing other children, and while he has always engaged in aggressive behaviors at home, aggression toward his 6-year-old brother has increased in the past few months.

Mark has always performed well at school; however, he has recently been struggling to maintain his grades in his math class, and has been having increasing difficulty with reading comprehension tasks. His teachers have also remarked that he frequently appears to be daydreaming, and will not complete classroom work without significant prompting. Similar behavior is reported when Mark is required to complete homework assignments. At school, Mark is fidgety while sitting at his desk, playing with pencils, shaking his legs, and tapping his fingers on the desk or on the chair repeatedly. His parents report that Mark has always engaged in aggressive behaviors, either hitting or pushing when he is upset or when plans changed unexpectedly; however, these behaviors have escalated both at home (with his brother) and at school. Mark is reported to yell and threaten other children at school when they do not engage in play the way he has told them to play, but this behavior has not escalated to hitting or pushing.

Results of a psychoeducational evaluation indicated that Mark's nonverbal skills were in the average range; however, his performance on nonverbal tasks indicated he had more difficulty with tasks that required organization of visual information, and timed tasks that required him to process information quickly. Mark's verbal skills were in the low end of the average range; his scores indicated that his ability to process verbal information was less well developed. Mark's overall cognitive functioning was in the average range. During testing Mark had difficulty remaining on task for long periods, and needed frequent redirecting.

Results of the ADOS-2 indicated social communication impairments (e.g., poor insight into relationships, difficulty maintaining conversations without direct questions). Several RRBs were observed during the testing including finger flicking, unusual sensory interests, and language (repeating phrases or sentences in the same way; repeating phrases heard from movies). Inflexibility with routines (insisting that play occurs in a specific way) was also evident. Impairments in attention, difficulty remaining on task, and difficulty completing tasks were observed across settings.

Based on this evaluation (which included multiple parent and teacher reports as well as other information), Mark met the diagnostic criteria for ASD, without intellectual disability and comorbid ADHD, inattentive type. Level of support required was substantial support for both social communication and restricted and repetitive behaviors.

Recommendations included ASD-specific socialization interventions to improve his weaknesses in social skills and social cognition. Goals of the social skills group should include increasing perspective-taking skills, problem-solving skills, turn-taking skills, sharing, and emotion recognition skills. Recommendations for his ADHD symptoms included consultation with a child psychiatrist with experience working with children with ASDs, PMT to help develop effective behavior management strategies in the home, and school consultation to implement supports for his inattention and behavioral concerns at school.

Treatment for ADHD began with consultation with a child and adolescent psychiatrist. Mark underwent a brief trial of a stimulant which resulted in increased irritability and aggression toward his brother and now peers, as well as social withdrawal and difficulty sleeping at night. Following clinical practice guidelines for treatment of ADHD symptoms in ASD from the Autism Speaks' Autism Treatment Network (ATN), his psychiatrist then started a trial with an alpha-agonist (guanfacine), and after some dosing adjustments, started to notice considerable improvements on parent and teacher reports of attention and compliance. In addition, his irritability and aggression toward peers at school was no longer an issue. However, he continues to have problems with regard to aggression toward his brother.

PMT and school consultation were the next steps of the intervention. Mark's parents enrolled in a 10-week PMT course at a local university clinic for children of parents with ADHD. They were unable to locate services for children with comorbid symptoms of ADHD and ASD. The course taught them several strategies to use at home to reinforce appropriate behaviors, including increasing use of praise (e.g., "catching them being good") and using a token economy that combined both positive reinforcement for target behaviors and punishments for aggression and yelling. After getting help in deciding appropriate target behaviors, reinforcements, and punishments, from the group therapy, the parents implemented the token economy at home. The token economy required adjustments over several weeks, but Mark's parents eventually found a system that worked for Mark and which was later adapted for his brother. The parents hired a private consultant to provide school consultation for lingering problems at school. The school consultant implemented a home-school communication note, a self-monitoring system to reward Mark for appropriate behaviors (e.g., sitting, asking for help), and a reward system tied to his home token economy.

The school consultation was reduced to once monthly check-ups after 3 months of more intensive services. In the next school year, the school consultant worked with Mark's teachers to ensure a smooth transition of behavior systems to the middle school setting. Mark continues to struggle with social skills impairments, needs some redirection for focusing, and is struggling with the independence required in middle school (e.g., organization, making many transitions). However, he is more attentive in class, more easily redirected, and has fewer struggles with his parents and sibling at home following the intervention plan described above.

4.1.10 Complementary and Alternative Medicine

CAM approaches are commonly used across medical and developmental conditions that are often used in conjunction with (or an alternative to) lengthy, intensive behavioral interventions (Warren, McPheeters, et al., 2011). Surveys on use of CAMs in the treatment of ASD suggest usage rates from 31.7% (Levy, Mandell, Merhar, Ittenbach, & Pinto-Martin, 2003) to 74% (Hanson et al., 2007). Greater use of CAM treatments is associated with particular patient and family characteristics including married couples, parents with graduate level education, and patients with more severe symptoms (based on parent ratings) (Hall & Riccio, 2012).

The category of CAM treatments in ASD includes biological treatments such as melatonin, vitamin supplementation, and chelation, as well as non-biological treatments such as auditory integration training, elimination diets, facilitated communication, and music therapy (see box below). The treatments range from commonly used programs from allied health disciplines (e.g., music or sensory integration therapy), animal-assisted therapies, and high-risk biomedical approaches (e.g., chelation). In addition to specific treatments, CAM treatment protocols for ASD have been developed. A widely known approach known as Defeat Autism Now! (DAN!) protocols involves training physicians to deliver assessment and treatment protocols focused on nontraditional treatment targets including immunotherapies, heavy metal detoxification, testing for hidden allergies, and nutritional supplements. To date, research has not been conducted on the DAN! protocol despite widespread use. In one survey, the most commonly used CAM approaches included gluten- and/or casein-free diets, secretin, omega-3 fatty acid supplementation, probiotics, glutathaione, specific carbohydrate diet, S-adenosylmethionine, and melatonin (Hall & Riccio, 2012).

Examples of CAM Treatments

1. **Biological CAM treatments**
   Melatonin
   Vitamin supplementation
   Chelation

2. **Nonbiological CAM treatments**
   Auditory integration training
   Elimination diets
   Facilitated communication
   Music therapy

The prominence of CAM treatment options complicates the clinical care of individuals with ASD in many ways. Significant resources (e.g., money and time) are often required to implement CAM treatments, as these treatments are often too complicated to be administered in standard educational and medical settings where individuals with ASD receive their care. Secondly, given the experimental nature of these treatments, many families may not feel comfortable sharing their choices to explore CAM with their primary care, mental health, or education service providers. To date, most CAM treatments have not been the subject of rigorous empirical investigation, impeding establishment (or not) of efficacy. However, a handful have demonstrated some evidence of efficacy for people with ASD in studies of varying levels of rigor, including use of melatonin for sleep problems in ASD and omega-3 supplementation for ADHD symptoms in ASD (Hendren, 2013; Warren, McPheeters, et al., 2011).

Biological CAM Treatments

The distinction between biological and nonbiological CAM treatments at times may be blurred by the biological hypotheses underlying several non-medical treatment approaches. The treatments described below are typically conducted under the auspices of medical professionals and may be based in emerging literature related to medical conditions associated with ASD (e.g., immune dysfunction). Treatments that have been discredited, such as secretin, will not be covered in detail here, given the strong evidence against efficacy (Williams, Wray, & Wheeler, 2005).

Melatonin

Melatonin is a widely used CAM for treating sleep problems in people with ASD (Malow et al., 2012). Melatonin appears to be one of the few CAM treatments with relatively positive support in the empirical literature for its use, particularly for improving problems with sleep onset and duration. Nighttime awakenings were not affected by melatonin treatment. Dosing ranged from 2 mg to 10 mg/night across 1.5 weeks to 3 months, and few side effects were reported across trials (Whitehouse, 2013).

Dietary Interventions

Dietary interventions are a popular alternative treatment approach

Dietary interventions are among the most popular alternative treatment approaches used with people with ASD. Dietary interventions include nutritional supplementation as well as elimination diets. Nutritional supplementation in ASD has included, but is not limited to, omega-3 fatty acid supplementation, methyl B12, probiotics, and multivitamin therapy (Hendren, 2013). Megavitamin therapies were among the earliest CAM treatments used. The rationale for megavitamin therapies lies in a presumption that nutrients impact neurotransmitter formation and function, and supplementation may facilitate normalization of neurotransmitter imbalances (e.g., serotonin) hypothesized to play a role in ASD. Vitamin B_6 is among the more popular and widely used nutritional supplements used with children with ASD, although controlled trials have not found it to be efficacious. The presence of side effects such as peripheral neuropathy (Romanczyk, Arnstein, Valluripalli, & Gillis, 2003) suggests the risks of treatment may outweigh the benefits. In contrast, research appears to support omega-3 supplementation (e.g., fish oil, primrose oil; Warren, Veenstra-Vanderweele, et al., 2011). The effectiveness of omega-3 and omega-6 fatty acid supplementation in ASD has also led to hypotheses of increased efficacy in the subset of children with ASD and comorbid ADHD.

Elimination diets are another widely used dietary intervention typically involving elimination of gluten and/or casein (i.e., gluten-free, casein-free [GFCF] diets); as well as food items that may have been found to challenge a child's system in standard skin prick tests. GFCF diets are based on views of ASD as a "leaky gut" syndrome. Leaky gut theories hypothesize that a host of diseases, particularly autoimmune diseases, may be caused by increased permeability of the intestinal lining. The increased intestinal permeability results in transmission of undesirable toxins and compounds across the blood–brain barrier to cause a host of disease states including ASD (Whitehouse, 2013). A review of elimination diets in ASD recently identified three of 14 studies as sufficiently well controlled to include in a review, and all three of these studies found little to no efficacy for elimination diets targeting gluten and/or casein (Mulloy et al., 2010).

In addition to the dietary interventions described above, several other biomedical interventions present with sufficient risk to warrant significant caution to families considering these treatments. High-risk CAM treatments previously used in ASD include chelation and immunotherapies. Chelation describes an approach drawn from treatments for heavy metal intoxication. The use of chelation in treating ASD is based on hypotheses that ASD is caused by heavy metal accumulation in the body, particularly mercury. Chelation treatments have often used dimercaptosuccinic acid (DMSA), which has been FDA approved to treat lead poisoning and has been widely used off-label in treatment of presumed mercury intoxication in ASD. An RCT did not find efficacy from one round of DMSA chelation (Adams et al., 2009). Side effects included diarrhea and fatigue and abnormal complete blood count, liver function tests, and mineral levels. In addition, gastrointestinal symptoms, regression, rashes, and sulfur smells were reported in some patients (Warren, Veenstra-Vanderweele, et al., 2011).

Several immunotherapies have also been evaluated in the treatment of ASD (Anagnostou & Hansen, 2011). These immunotherapies are conducted based on the growing body of data suggesting immune dysregulation as well as susceptibility to autoimmune disorders in individuals with ASD. Despite the growth in research on associated conditions in ASD that provides evidence for altered immune system functioning, research on immunotherapies has been very limited, and substantially more rigorous investigations are required regarding safety and efficacy.

Nonbiological CAM Treatments

There have been multiple nonbiological treatments that are commonly used in the treatment of ASD. Nonbiological treatments include allied health treatments such as music therapy, sensory integration therapy, auditory integration therapy, massage therapy, acupuncture, and animal-assisted therapies (e.g., therapeutic horse riding, dolphin therapy). This group of treatments represents interventions that have not been sufficiently tested, such as music therapy and some animal-assisted therapies, as well as treatments that have been evaluated and shown to be nonefficacious (e.g., facilitated communication).

Two nonbiological CAM approaches with emerging, but still limited data for their efficacy are music and therapeutic horse riding. Music therapy is a popular nonbiological CAM which has generated interest given clinical observations of enhanced attention and engagement with music in people with ASD. Music therapy is believed to promote nonverbal, verbal, and social communication in children with ASD. Music therapy has been studied in one RCT in preschoolers, showing positive effects on joint attention and eye contact on

Music therapy focuses on promoting nonverbal, verbal, and social-communication

a standardized measure of early symptoms of autism (Kim, Wigram, & Gold, 2009).

Animal-assisted therapies are also commonly used to target a wide spectrum of symptoms including cognitive, social, and sensory impairments. Few data exist documenting the effectiveness of animal-assisted therapies. However, one commonly used animal-assisted therapy, therapeutic horse riding (also known as hippotherapy) was evaluated in an RCT using a wait-list control group and unblinded parent report of behavior. Results indicated that children in the horse-riding group were rated as significantly more improved on the Sensory Profile (Dunn, 1999) and a measure of autism symptom severity (Constantino & Gruber, 2005) compared with the wait-list control group (Bass, Duchowny, & Llabre, 2009).

Auditory integration training (AIT) and sensory integration training (SIT) are widely used treatments targeting underlying sensory processing impairments in ASD. In AIT, hyperacusis in ASD is treated through presenting filtered music according to the specific protocols and individual patient profiles over several sessions. Exposure to filtered sounds within the systematic protocol is believed to reduce hypersensitivity to noise, improve behavior, and enhance social skills. Three RCTs found improvements in both AIT and "placebo" (e.g., unfiltered sounds) groups on standardized behavior rating scales (Bettison, 1996; Mudford et al., 2000). These findings are in contrast to less well-designed trials suggesting behavioral improvements resulting from AIT, and the findings also suggested that AIT yielded some negative side effects including increases in behavior problems (e.g., aggression), sleep disturbance, headaches, and stomachaches (Bettison, 1996; Edelson et al., 1999). SIT is believed to address both hypersensitivity and hyposensitivity to sensory stimuli in people with ASD. While the link between specific treatment components and underlying neurobiology is not fully described, SIT uses a variety of stimuli to facilitate normalized processing of vestibular, tactile, and proprioceptive stimuli (Romanczyk et al., 2003). Sensory stimulation is typically facilitated through an environment that allows self-directed exploration of stimuli and games that challenge the sensory system. These may include strategies such as brushing skin and compressing the child between mats for tactile stimulation; swinging, balance balls, riding on scooter boards on the stomach for proprioceptive training, and swinging for vestibular stimulation. To date, too few studies of acceptable quality are available to evaluate the efficacy of SIT, despite its widespread use (Warren, McPheeters et al., 2011). See Appendix 1 for further reading on ASD inverventions.

4.2   Mechanisms of Action

Research on the phenomenology and treatment of ASD remains a relatively young field of investigation. Early intervention programs and behavioral reduction programs are firmly grounded in operant conditioning models of learning and memory which are among the research domains in the behavioral sciences with the strongest evidence. A similar rationale underlies adaptations of CBT programs for comorbid anxiety disorders in people with ASD, with extinction learning as a central mechanism in the treatment paradigm. However, few studies of educational and psychosocial treatments for people with ASD have been designed to evaluate potential mechanisms of treatment effects. For some treatments with several promising, validated models (e.g., EIBIs), future research would benefit from a focus on identifying common elements and mechanisms of change.

Mechanistic research is critical to isolating common elements across treatments, developing personalized interventions, informing research on combinations/variations, and dissemination. However, since mechanisms of action are typically explored only after efficacy has been established, this limits the research on this topic in ASD. In ASD research, moderators and mediators of change have been explored for some psychosocial interventions, and some potential factors have been suggested. In a review of psychosocial interventions (CBT and social skills training), Lerner, White, and McPartland (2012) discuss the potential mechanistic impact of decreasing disruptive behaviors, using social motivation, and targeting improvement in executive functioning in order to improve social skills. These potential mechanisms, however, have not been systematically reviewed across treatment studies, although they have been documented in naturalistic and experimental designs.

With respect to mechanisms of action for pharmacotherapies for ASD, there is very little research with respect to any proven therapy for core ASD symptoms, since efficacy has not been established. However, with respect to therapies showing efficacy for associated features, as those described throughout this work, it is not within the scope of this book to discuss mechanisms of action for these features that relate to targets other than ASD (e.g., stimulants for symptoms of inattention). Mechanisms for enhancing and expediting derailed developmental trajectories in social communication, essential for targeting core ASD symptoms, may include plasticity and changes to synapse morphology, creating a better learning environment in which educational/behavioral interventions can be maximized (Castrén, Elgersma, Maffei, & Hagerman, 2012).

4.3   Efficacy and Prognosis

Intervention is the second strongest area of growth in ASD research, experiencing an approximately fivefold increase since 2000 and preceded only by research on etiology (Office of Autism Research Coordination et al., 2012). The growth in treatment research has led to increased methodological rigor. However, early debates in ASD treatment research mirrored those that took place in the broader field of clinical psychology, including debates on the appropriateness of testing psychosocial treatments (e.g., educational, therapy) using RCT designs. The argument against RCTs was made early on regarding educational, specifically ABA, treatments, which were based in behavior analytic traditions using single-subject experimental designs. Today, single-subject experimental designs are valued as an important methodological step in the treatment development process, and are recommended particularly in the early stages of treatment development to test methods and hypotheses, prior to initiating expensive RCTs.

The advances made in treatment research as well as the demand for evidence-based interventions for people with ASD are reflected in the recent publication of several best practice reviews (see Chapter 5: Further Reading). Each report outlines distinct but related criteria for determining the quality of the evidence base, as well as terminology for categorizing interventions by level and quality of empirical support.

While the criteria and conclusions differ widely, the reviews provide a consensus on the support for treatments based in behavior analytic traditions including EIBIs such as DTT as well as behavior reduction approaches (e.g., FBA).

Another important trend in research is the systematic evaluation of popular CAM treatments. Positive reports of therapeutic horseback riding and music therapy have been published (Bass, Duchowny, & Llabre, 2009; Kim, Wigram, & Gold, 2009). Both trials were small and reported effects on unblinded parent reports, but they represent an important step toward accumulating data for widely used therapeutic approaches. In contrast, other alternative treatments, such as facilitated communication and secretin, have been evaluated in well-controlled studies and have been shown to be ineffective; these studies provide strong support for families and clinicians seeking data to inform clinical decision making. Several other popular treatments such as sensory integration and biomedically driven medication and supplements protocols (e.g., DAN protocols) have achieved significant popular support but have yet to be systematically and scientifically evaluated.

The varying approaches and conclusions from recent reviews reflect the need for continued investigation of evidence-based treatments for people with ASD across the lifespan. Methodological issues include the need for standardizing outcomes across trials, using measures that capture clinically meaningful outcomes, improving methodology related to treatment fidelity, and the need for RCTs to use active treatment controls (compared with waitlist or placebo controls). In addition, focusing on the educational, vocational, and mental health needs of older individuals with ASD is also a high priority for the field.

Finally, while we know that ASD is a neurodevelopmental disorder that changes throughout the lifetime, we most certainly do not know what the length of an efficacious treatment regimen should be, both for behavioral and pharmacological interventions (or the combination of the two). For instance, if the treatment begins to fail after a period of success, is that due to a lack of efficacy of the treatment, or a changing clinical profile that requires reevaluation of optimal treatments. Such consistent reevaluation of treatments is necessary when new core (e.g., a new ritual) or comorbid (e.g., development of seizure activity) symptoms develop. In fact, it has been speculated that some of the treatment trials that have "failed" may actually have not produced efficacious results because of heterogeneity between patients who were the focus of treatment targets (if there is a wide age range in the study sample, for instance), as well as because of developmental changes that may occur within an individual to change the course of treatment efficacy.

4.4   Variations and Combinations of Methods

Naturalistic behavior therapies were developed to address concerns regarding the spontaneity and generalizability of skills taught using DTT models of ABA. Naturalistic behavior therapy models may be used as an adjunct to DTT models to promote generalization or as a stand-alone therapy (e.g., PRT). The development of naturalistic behavior therapies has led to increased enthusiasm and dissemination, as demonstrated by recent comparative effectiveness trials (Smith et al., 2010). Continued research on variations of ABA and other comprehensive treatment models is needed to identify optimal "dosing" (e.g., individual; small group), training requirements for treatment providers, and translation to community settings.

Treatment research in ASD is a rapidly evolving field as demonstrated by the variations of treatment models for associated symptoms. For example, ASD-specific treatments for anxiety disorder may use a focused CBT manual or may use a modular approach incorporating elements of social skills training relevant to treatment goals (e.g., Wood et al., 2009). Similar variability is observed in socialization interventions for verbal, school-aged children with ASD. Treatment variables such as modality (group vs. individual), treatment targets, length of treatment, delivery system (e.g., clinic, school), and family involvement also contribute to the variations in methods reported in prior sections. As seen in other disorders as well as in studies of comprehensive educational programs, variations based on hypothesized mechanisms are likely to emerge as research on short-term focused interventions matures.

Combining treatments is a common practice, with combinations changing throughout the lifespan. To date, research has not addressed practice and research questions with regard to combinations of treatments. Questions regarding the selection, timing, targets, and sequencing of medication vs. psychotherapy remain largely unanswered for the various available treatments for individuals with ASD.

In addition, although combining of multiple behavioral and often multiple pharmacological treatments in ASD is the rule and not the exception, treatment research on combined treatments is limited to one large-scale trial evaluating the combination of PMT with risperidone and its impact on disruptive behaviors in children with ASD. In the design of the combined treatment trial, risperidone and PMT were hypothesized to target distinct behaviors presenting in children with high levels of irritability and aggression (Aman et al., 2009). Specifically, risperidone was hypothesized to facilitate reductions in aggression, tantrums, and self-injury, while PMT was believed to facilitate improved compliance and adaptive skill development. That multisite study evaluated PMT alone, PMT with medication (i.e., combined therapy), or medication alone (Aman et al., 2009). PMT was tailored to individuals with ASD through inclusion of visual schedules, FCT, and training adaptive skills, and focused on treating problem behaviors in a diverse sample of children with pervasive developmental disorders, although the majority presented with intellectual disabilities. Findings favored the combination treatment over the monotherapy condition. Participants in the combined treatment condition demonstrated greater improvements after 6 months of treatment (approximately 11 sessions). Outcomes included a measure of problem behaviors at home and on

Aberrant Behavior Checklist (Aman, Singh, Stewart, & Field, 1985), a widely used measure of associated and core symptoms in ASD clinical trials. Similar research evaluating effective interventions for other comorbid psychiatric symptoms (e.g., anxiety) and core symptoms is needed to help develop more individualized treatment approaches and practice parameters guiding interventions for this heterogeneous syndrome.

4.5   Problems in Carrying Out the Treatments

ASD treatments often cross disciplines and require implementation across multiple setting types

ASD is a disorder with pervasive impact. It presents early in development and typically persists throughout the lifetime. Since comorbidity with intellectual disability and other disorders affecting functioning is more often present than not, treatment regimens to optimally improve functioning often involve multiple components, and require frequent evaluation and reevaluation. Due to these elements, and in light of the varying types of educational and health care systems and settings, treatments for ASD often cross disciplines and require implementation across multiple setting types (e.g., school, private clinics, health care settings). It is difficult to overstate the importance of coordination of services for individuals with ASD throughout their lifetime.

In early childhood, while early intervention programs (in the United States) are often designed to be home-based and comprehensive in nature (including special education components as well as speech therapy, occupational therapy, and physical therapy) and are provided through a comprehensive individualized family service plan, families often seek additional therapies for young children with ASD that are outside of the scope of these plans, including variants of ABA or other comprehensive treatment models. In school-age years, while a significant portion of a child's treatment may occur within the scope of the educational system, ancillary treatments such as medication management, complementary and alternative treatments, and specific behavioral interventions are often not coordinated through this plan. In adulthood, service provision is further complicated by additional factors that include vocational and residential setting placements as well as standard therapies in which the individual may engage. Adults transition out of the educational system, thus service provision is implemented through other systems.

Integration and coordination of these multiple and changing service provision complexities for individuals with ASD, due to its nature involving life-long impairments and related disabilities, are listed as priorities in the strategic plan for autism research (Interagency Autism Coordinating Committee, 2012) and particularly with respect to the growing needs of the increasing adult population of individuals with ASD.

4.6   Multicultural Issues

While research suggests ASD rates generally do not differ according to culture, race, or ethnicity, studies have found significant differences in diagnostic practices according to race in the United States. Globally, the interconnected factors of parenting practices, societal attitudes toward education and health care, availability of resources, policies and practices of regions and countries, and societal and political perspectives on mental health can influence how and when disorders such as ASD are diagnosed, and how ASD is thereafter treated.

The impact of culture on parenting practices starts early. Which developmental milestones receive attention and how developmental milestones are understood, measured, and interpreted are all connected to culture. For example, when measured systematically, the play practices of typically developing young Korean-American children were found to differ from those of White-American children; Korean-American children were reported to engage in less social and pretend play (Farver & Lee-Shin, 2000). Similarly, cultural differences may also affect the timing and types of symptoms that are recognized. For instance, while many US studies find language delay to be the first symptom discussed with professionals when ASD is later diagnosed, one study indicated that in India, almost 50% of families noticed social interaction symptoms earlier than communication delays in children who were later diagnosed with ASD (Daley, 2004). These differences can have a major impact on which children are diagnosed with ASD, as well as when and why they are diagnosed.

On a societal level, political and cultural perspectives on child development and mental health can affect the understanding of a disorder, as well as the help-seeking behavior that ensues once developmental concerns emerge. While not conducting any systematic epidemiological study, anthropologist Roy Richard Grinker has written extensively about cultural differences and changes in culture that may have influenced the increase in ASD diagnosis both in the United States and abroad (Grinker, 2007).

Grinker and others have noted that most research on the influence of culture and related demographic differences in ASD has been tightly linked to the issues of initial identification and diagnosis of the disorder, which relates to later provision of interventions and services. Understanding the early signs of delayed development, and ASD specifically, has been prioritized by health agencies in the United States, Canada, and Europe, and health campaigns have targeted teaching recognition of typical and atypical development in young children. With these educational and resource programs in place, children have been diagnosed early, and they have been provided with intervention and services in the early stages of development.

Racial and ethnic disparities exist and influence when diagnosis occurs as well as the type and amount of intervention

Despite the numerous gains in early identification (and therefore early intervention), racial and ethnic disparities exist and influence when racial and ethnic minorities are diagnosed, as well as the type and amount of intervention that minority groups receive (Feinberg et al., 2011; Mandell et al., 2002). Providers' understanding and awareness of cultural differences have also been demonstrated to have an impact on minority families; for instance, one study indicated that in the United States, African American parents reported that family physicians did not provide enough care, nor did they provide culturally sensitive care to their children with ASD (Montes & Halterman, 2007).

The impact of race and culture on parental perception and coping is another important aspect. A recent study found that race plays a role in a mother's perception of the negative impact of their children's ASD symptoms on their lives. Interestingly, this longitudinal study reported that in the United States, African American mothers with lower levels of education reported being less troubled by having a child with ASD than African American mothers with higher levels of education and all White mothers (Carr & Lord, 2013).

In the United States, it has been challenging to study racial, ethnic, and cultural differences in ASD because of small sample sizes and the fact that research samples are often homogenous. The possible impact of race, ethnicity, and culture on outcome is undoubtedly important to examine, and research on the impact of these factors on the outcome of ASD interventions is beginning to emerge. A study examining race and ethnicity factors on the outcomes for children receiving PRT indicated no differences between Hispanic, White, Asian, and African American groups (Baker-Ericzen, Stahmer, & Burns, 2007). Overall, however, evidence-based research on culture, race, and ethnicity in ASD remains sparse and is important to address as the field moves forward.

4.7   Future Directions for ASD Treatment

The ultimate goal for ASD treatment is remediation of the disorder. However, we have not been able to achieve this goal, although steps have been taken to improve functioning for many individual children.

Owing to the shift toward a more "personalized medicine" approach to treatment, it is now common to individualize or "tailor" treatments to the specific profile of each child. Such tailoring will require consideration of behavioral strengths and weaknesses of individuals, and we are now beginning to understand that an individual's biology and genetics profile includes important treatment variables.

Future Directions: Optimizing combinations of behavioral interventions with medications for core symptom domains

Since ASD is associated with many known (and presumably, as-yet-unidentified) genetic abnormalities, we now know that treatments should target the behavioral as well as neurobiological profiles of individuals with ASD. In addition to personalizing pharmaceutical approaches based on profiles of symptoms and associated conditions, future directions for optimizing treatment for ASD will also include optimizing combinations of behavioral interventions with medications. A recent example includes a RUPP trial evaluating efficacy of PMT with pharmacological approaches for disruptive behaviors in ASD (Aman, et al., 2009). Hypothesis-driven targeted combined interventions for core symptom impairments will be important future directions for intervention development research in ASD. However, such work will need to be undertaken without stalling implementation/services research. Evaluating and delivering effective, targeted treatments particularly for underdiagnosed and undertreated subgroups remains a formidable challenge for the field.

5

Further Reading

National Autism Center. (2009). *National standards report: Addressing the need for evidence-based practice guidelines for autism spectrum disorders.* Randolph, MA: Author. Retrieved from http://www.nationalautismcenter.org/pdf/NAC%20Standards%20Report.pdf
This publication provides a review of the existing evidence for treatments and educational interventions for individuals with ASD.

Vismara, L. A., & Rogers, S. J. (2010). Behavioral treatments in autism spectrum disorder: What do we know? *Annual Review of Clinical Psychology, 6*, 447–468.
Research paper that describes and reviews different behavioral treatment interventions for children and adolescents with ASD.

Warren, Z., McPheeters, M. L., Sathe, N., Foss-Feig, J. H., Glasser, A., & Veenstra-Vanderweele, J. (2011). A systematic review of early intensive intervention for autism spectrum disorders. *Pediatrics, 127*(5), 1303–1311.
Research paper reviewing early interventions for children with ASD.

Warren, Z., Veenstra-Vanderweele, J., Stone, W., Bruzek, J. L., Nahmias, A. S., Foss-Feig, J. H., ... McPheeters, M. L. (2011). Therapies for children with autism spectrum disorders (Report No. 11-EHC029-EF). *Comparative Effectiveness Review No. 26*. Rockville, MD: Agency for Healthcare Research and Quality. Retrieved from http://www.ncbi.nlm.nih.gov/books/NBK56343/
Comprehensive review of therapies and interventions for children with ASD.

6

References

Abikoff, H. B., Jensen, P. S., Arnold, L. L., Hoza, B., Hechtman, L., Pollack, S., ... Wigal, T. (2002). Observed classroom behavior of children with ADHD: Relationship to gender and comorbidity. *Journal of Abnormal Child Psychology, 30*(4), 349–359. doi: 10.1023/A:1015713807297

Adams, J. B., Baral, M., Geis, E., Mitchell, J., Ingram, J., Hensley, A., ... El-Dahr, J. (2009). Safety and efficacy of oral DMSA therapy for children with autism spectrum disorders. Part B: Behavioral results. *BMC Clinical Pharmacology, 9*, 17. doi: 10.1186/1472-6904-9-16

Aman, M. G., Lam, K. S., & Van Bourgondien, M. E. (2005). Medication patterns in patients with autism: Temporal, regional, and demographic influences. *Journal of Child and Adolescent Psychopharmacology, 15*(1), 116–126. doi: 10.1089/cap.2005.15.116

Aman, M. G., McDougle, C. J., Scahill, L., Handen, B., Arnold, L. E., Johnson, C., ... Wagner, A. (2009). Medication and parent training in children with pervasive developmental disorders and serious behavior problems: Results from a randomized clinical trial. *Journal of the American Academy of Child and Adolescent Psychiatry, 48*(12), 1143–1154. doi: 10.1097/CHI.0b013e3181bfd669

Aman, M. G., Singh, N. N., Stewart, A. W., & Field, C. J. (1985). The aberrant behavior checklist: A behavior rating scale for the assessment of treatment effects. *American Journal of Mental Deficiency, 89*(5), 485–491.

APA – American Psychiatric Association. (1968). *Diagnostic and statistical manual of mental disorders* (2nd ed.). Washington, DC: Author.

APA – American Psychiatric Association. (1980). *Diagnostic and statistical manual of mental disorders* (3rd ed.). Washington, DC: Author.

APA – American Psychiatric Association. (1987). *Diagnostic and statistical manual of mental disorders* (3rd ed., text revision). Washington, DC: Author.

APA – American Psychiatric Association. (1994). *Diagnostic and statistical manual of mental disorders* (4th ed.). Washington, DC: Author.

APA – American Psychiatric Association. (2000). *Diagnostic and statistical manual of mental disorders* (4th ed., text rev.). Washington, DC: Author.

APA – American Psychiatric Association. (2013). *Diagnostic and statistical manual of mental disorders* (5th ed.). Arlington, VA: American Psychiatric Publishing.

Anagnostou, E., & Hansen, R. (2011). Medical treatment overview: Traditional and novel psycho-pharmacological and complementary and alternative medications. *Current Opinions in Pediatrics, 23*(6), 621–627. doi: 10.1097/MOP.0b013e32834cba3e

Anderson, D. K., Lord, C., Risi, S., DiLavore, P. S., Shulman, C., Thurm, A., ... Pickles, A. (2007). Patterns of growth in verbal abilities among children with autism spectrum disorder. *Journal of Consulting and Clinical Psychology, 75*(4), 594–604. doi: 10.1037/0022-006X.75.4.594

Apple, A. L., Billingsley, F., Schwartz, I. S., & Carr, E. G. (2005). Effects of video modeling alone and with self-management on compliment-giving behaviors of children with high-functioning ASD. *Journal of Positive Behavior Interventions, 7*(1), 33–46. doi: 10.1177/10983007050070010401

Asperger, H., & Frith, U. (1991). 'Autistic psychopathy' in childhood. In U. Frith (Ed.), *Autism and Asperger syndrome* (pp. 37–92). New York, NY: Cambridge University Press. doi: 10.1017/CBO9780511526770.002

Baker, J. P. (2010). Autism in 1959: Joey the mechanical boy. *Pediatrics, 125*(6), 1101–1103. doi: 10.1542/peds.2010-0846

Baker-Ericzen, M. J., Stahmer, A., & Burns, A. (2007). Child demographics associated with outcomes in a community-based Pivotal Response Training program. *Journal of Positive Behavior Interventions, 9*, 52–60. doi: 10.1177/10983007070090010601

Baron-Cohen, S., Allen, J., & Gillberg, C. (1992). Can autism be detected at 18 months? The needle, the haystack, and the CHAT. *British Journal of Psychiatry, 161*, 839–843. doi: 10.1192/bjp.161.6.839

Baron-Cohen, S., Wheelwright, S., Skinner, R., Martin, J., & Clubley, E. (2001). The autism-spectrum quotient (AQ): Evidence from Asperger syndrome/high-functioning autism, males and females, scientists and mathematicians. *Journal of Autism and Developmental Disorders, 31*(1), 5–17. doi: 10.1023/A:1005653411471

Bass, M., Duchowny, C., & Llabre, M. (2009). The effect of therapeutic horseback riding on social functioning in children with autism. *Journal of Autism and Developmental Disorders, 39*(9), 1261–1267. doi: 10.1007/s10803-009-0734-3

Begeer, S., Mandell, D., Wijnker-Holmes, B., Venderbosch, S., Rem, D., Stekelenburg, F., & Koot, H. M. (2013). Sex differences in the timing of identification among children and adults with autism spectrum disorders. *Journal of Autism and Developmental Disorders, 43*(5), 1151–1156. doi:10.1007/s10803-012-1656-z

Behrens, M. L., & Goldfarb, W. (1958). A study of patterns of interaction of families of schizophrenic children in residential treatment. *American Journal of Orthopsychiatry, 28*(2), 300–312. doi: 10.1111/j.1939-0025.1958.tb03749.x

Bettelheim, B. (1967). *The empty fortress: Infantile autism and the birth of the self.* New York, NY: Free Press.

Bettison, S. (1996). The long-term effects of auditory training on children with autism. *Journal of Autism and Developmental Disorders, 26*(3), 361–374. doi: 10.1007/BF02172480

Bodfish, J. W., Symons, F. J., Parker, D. E., & Lewis, M. H. (2000). Varieties of repetitive behavior in autism: Comparisons to mental retardation. *Journal of Autism and Developmental Disorders, 30*(3), 237–243. doi: 10.1023/A:1005596502855

Bondy, A. S., & Frost, L. A. (1998). The picture exchange communication system. *Seminars in Speech and Language, 19*(4), 373–388. doi: 10.1055/s-2008-1064055

Bourret, J., Vollmer, T. R., & Rapp, J. T. (2004). Evaluation of a vocal mand assessment and vocal mand training procedures. *Journal of Applied Behavior Analysis, 37*(2), 129–143. doi: 10.1901/jaba.2004.37-129

Bramham, J., Ambery, F., Young, S., Morris, R., Russell, A., Xenitidis, K., … Murphy, D. (2009). Executive functioning differences between adults with attention deficit hyperactivity disorder and autistic spectrum disorder in initiation, planning and strategy formation. *Autism, 13*(3), 245–264. doi: 10.1177/1362361309103790

Broder-Fingert, S., Shui, A., Pulcini, C. D., Kurowski, D., & Perrin, J. M. (2013). Racial and ethnic differences in subspecialty service use by children with autism. *Pediatrics, 132*(1), 94–100. doi: 10.1542/peds.2012-3886

Brooks-Kayal, A. (2010). Epilepsy and autism spectrum disorders: Are there common developmental mechanisms? *Brain Development, 32*(9), 731–738. doi: 10.1016/j.braindev.2010.04.010

Campbell, D. B., Buie, T. M., Winter, H., Bauman, M., Sutcliffe, J. S., Perrin, J. M., & Levitt, P. (2009). Distinct genetic risk based on association of MET in families with co-occurring autism and gastrointestinal conditions. *Pediatrics, 123*(3), 1018–1024. doi: 10.1542/peds.2008-0819

Carr, T., & Lord, C. (2013). Longitudinal study of perceived negative impact in African American and Caucasian mothers of children with autism spectrum disorder. *Autism, 17*(4), 405–417. doi: 10.1177/1362361311435155

Carter, M., & Scherer, S. (2013). Autism spectrum disorder in the genetics clinic: A review. *Clinical Genetics, 83*(5), 399–407. doi: 10.1111/cge.12101

Castrén, E., Elgersma, Y., Maffei, L., & Hagerman, R. (2012). Treatment of neurodevelopmental disorders in adulthood. *Journal of Neuroscience, 32*(41), 14074–14079. doi: 10.1523/JNEUROSCI.3287-12.2012

Charlop-Christy, M. H., Carpenter, M., Le, L., LeBlanc, L. A., & Kellet, K. (2002). Using the picture exchange communication system (PECS) with children with autism: Assessment of PECS acquisition, speech, social-communicative behavior, and problem behavior. *Journal of Applied Behavior Analysis, 35*(3), 213–231. doi: 10.1901/jaba.2002.35-213

Charman, T., Baird, G., Simonoff, E., Loucas, T., Chandler, S., Meldrum, D., & Pickles, A. (2007). Efficacy of three screening instruments in the identification of autistic-spectrum disorders. *British Journal of Psychiatry, 191*, 554–559. doi: 10.1192/bjp.bp.107.040196

Charman, T., Pickles, A., Simonoff, E., Chandler, S., Loucas, T., & Baird, G. (2011). IQ in children with autism spectrum disorders: Data from the Special Needs and Autism Project (SNAP). *Psychological Medicine, 41*(3), 619–627. doi: 10.1017/S0033291710000991

Charman, T., Taylor, E., Drew, A., Cockerill, H., Brown, J. A., & Baird, G. (2005). Outcome at 7 years of children diagnosed with autism at age 2: Predictive validity of assessments conducted at 2 and 3 years of age and pattern of symptom change over time. *Journal of Child Psychology and Psychiatry, 46*(5), 500–513. doi: 10.1111/j.1469-7610.2004.00377.x

Chaste, P., & Leboyer, M. (2012). Autism risk factors: Genes, environment, and gene-environment interactions. *Dialogues in Clinical Neuroscience, 14*(3), 281–292.

Chevallier, C., Kohls, G., Troiani, V., Brodkin, E. S., & Schultz, R. T. (2012). The social motivation theory of autism. *Trends in Cognitive Sciences, 16*(4), 231–239. doi: 10.1016/j.tics.2012.02.007

Chronis, A. M., Jones, H. A., & Raggi, V. L. (2006). Evidence-based psychosocial treatments for children and adolescents with attention-deficit/hyperactivity disorder. *Clinical Psychology Review, 26*(4), 486–502. doi: 10.1016/j.cpr.2006.01.002

Clerk, G. (1961). Reflections on the role of the mother in the development of language in the schizophrenic child. *Canadian Psychiatric Association Journal, 6*, 252–256.

Clifford, S. M., & Dissanayake, C. (2008). The early development of joint attention in infants with autistic disorder using home video observations and parental interview. *Journal of Autism and Developmental Disorders, 38*(5), 791–805. doi: 10.1007/s10803-007-0444-7

Cohen, I. L., Schmidt-Lackner, S., Romanczyk, R., & Sudhalter, V. (2003). The PDD Behavior Inventory: A rating scale for assessing response to intervention in children with pervasive developmental disorder. *Journal of Autism and Developmental Disorders, 33*(1), 31–45. doi: 10.1023/A:1022278420716

Constantino, J. N., & Gruber, C. P. (2005). *Social Responsiveness Scale.* Los Angeles, CA: Western Psychological Services.

Corsello, C., Hus, V., Pickles, A., Risi, S., Cook, E. H., Jr., Leventhal, B. L., & Lord, C. (2007). Between a ROC and a hard place: Decision making and making decisions about using the SCQ. *Journal of Child Psychology and Psychiatry, 48*(9), 932–940. doi: 10.1111/j.1469-7610.2007.01762.x

Coury, D. L., Anagnostou, E., Manning-Courtney, P., Reynolds, A., Cole, L., McCoy, R., … Perrin, J. M. (2012). Use of psychotropic medication in children and adolescents with autism spectrum disorders. *Pediatrics, 130*(Suppl 2), S69–S76. doi: 10.1542/peds.2012-0900D

Cox, A., Rutter, M., Newman, S., & Bartak, L. (1975). A comparative study of infantile autism and specific developmental receptive language disorder. II. Parental characteristics. *British Journal of Psychiatry, 126*, 146–159. doi: 10.1192/bjp.126.2.146

Creak, M., & Pampiglione, G. (1969). Clinical and EEG studies on a group of 35 psychotic children. *Developmental Medicine and Child Neurology, 11*(2), 218–227. doi: 10.1111/j.1469-8749.1969.tb01420.x

Daley, T. C. (2004). From symptom recognition to diagnosis: children with autism in urban India. *Social Science and Medicine, 58*, 1323–1335. doi: 10.1016/S0277-9536(03)00330-7

Davis, T. E., 3rd, Moree, B. N., Dempsey, T., Hess, J. A., Jenkins, W. S., Fodstad, J. C., & Matson, J. L. (2012). The effect of communication deficits on anxiety symptoms in infants and toddlers with autism spectrum disorders. *Behavior Therapy, 43*(1), 142–152. doi: 10.1016/j.beth.2011.05.003

Dawson, G., Meltzoff, A. N., Osterling, J., Rinaldi, J., & Brown, E. (1998). Children with autism fail to orient to naturally occurring social stimuli. *Journal of Autism and Developmental Disorders, 28*(6), 479–485. doi: 10.1023/A:1026043926488

Dawson, G., Rogers, S., Munson, J., Smith, M., Winter, J., Greenson, J., … Varley, J. (2010). Randomized, controlled trial of an intervention for toddlers with autism: The early start Denver model. *Pediatrics, 125*(1), e17–e23. doi: 10.1542/peds.2009-0958

Denham, S. A., Blair, K. A., DeMulder, E., Levitas, J., Sawyer, K., Auerbach-Major, S., & Queenan, P. (2003). Preschool emotional competence: Pathway to social competence? *Child Development, 74*(1), 238–256. doi: 10.1111/1467-8624.00533

DeRosier, M., Swick, D., Davis, N., McMillen, J., & Matthews, R. (2011). The efficacy of a social skills group intervention for improving social behaviors in children with high functioning autism spectrum disorders. *Journal of Autism and Developmental Disorders, 41*(8), 1033–1043. doi: 10.1007/s10803-010-1128-2

Doyle, C. A., & McDougle, C. J. (2012). Pharmacologic treatments for the behavioral symptoms associated with autism spectrum disorders across the lifespan. *Dialogues in Clinical Neuroscience, 14*(3), 263–279.

Dunn, W. (1999). *Sensory profile: User's manual.* San Antonio, TX: Psychological Corporation.

Durand, V. M., & Carr, E. G. (1991). Functional communication training to reduce challenging behavior: Maintenance and application in new settings. *Journal of Applied Behavior Analysis, 24*(2), 251–264. doi: 10.1901/jaba.1991.24-251

Eaves, L. C., & Ho, H. H. (2008). Young adult outcome of autism spectrum disorders. *Journal of Autism and Developmental Disorders, 38*(4), 739–747. doi: 10.1007/s10803-007-0441-x

Edelson, S. M., Arin, D., Bauman, M., Lukas, S. E., Rudy, J. H., Sholar, M., & Rimland, B. (1999). Auditory integration training: A double-blind study of behavioral and electrophysiological effects in people with autism. *Focus on Autism and Other Developmental Disabilities, 14*(2), 73–81. doi: 10.1177/108835769901400202

Esbensen, A. J., Greenberg, J. S., Seltzer, M. M., & Aman, M. G. (2009). A longitudinal investigation of psychotropic and non-psychotropic medication use among adolescents and adults with autism spectrum disorders. *Journal of Autism and Developmental Disorders, 39*(9), 1339–1349. doi: 10.1007/s10803-009-0750-3

Farmer, C., Thurm, A., & Grant, P. (2013). Pharmacotherapy for the core symptoms in autistic disorder: Current status of the research. *Drugs, 73*(4), 303–314. doi: 10.1007/s40265-013-0021-7

Farver, J. A., & Lee-Shin, Y. (2000). Acculturation and Korean-American children's social and play behavior. *Social Development, 9*, 316–336. doi: 10.1111/1467-9507.00128

Feinberg, E., Silverstein, M., Donahue, S., & Bliss, R. (2011). The impact of race on participation in part c early intervention services. *Journal of Developmental Behavioral Pediatrics, 32*(4), 284–291. doi: 10.1097/DBP.0b013e3182142fbd

Fombonne, E., Quirke, S., & Hagen, A. (2011). Epidemiology of pervasive developmental disorders. In D. G. Amaral, G. Dawson, & D. H. Geschwind (Eds.), *Autism spectrum disorders* (pp. 90–111). New York, NY: Oxford University Press. doi: 10.1093/med/9780195371826.003.0007

Fountain, C., Winter, A. S., & Bearman, P. S. (2012). Six developmental trajectories characterize children with autism. *Pediatrics, 129*(5), e1112–e1120. doi: 10.1542/peds.2011-1601

Frankel, F., Myatt, R., Sugar, C., Whitham, C., Gorospe, C. M., & Laugeson, E. (2010). A randomized controlled study of parent-assisted Children's Friendship Training with children having autism spectrum disorders. *Journal of Autism and Developmental Disorders, 40*(7), 827–842. doi: 10.1007/s10803-010-1016-9

Frith, U. (1989). Autism and "theory of mind." In C. Gillberg (Ed.), *Diagnosis and treatment of autism* (pp. 33–52). New York, NY: Plenum Press.

Frith, U. (1996). Cognitive explanations of autism. *Acta Paediatrica Supplement, 416*, 63–68. doi: 10.1111/j.1651-2227.1996.tb14280.x

Gadow, K. D., DeVincent, C. J., & Pomeroy, J. (2006). ADHD symptom subtypes in children with pervasive developmental disorder. *Journal of Autism and Developmental Disorders, 36*(2), 271–283. doi: 10.1007/s10803-005-0060-3

Gantman, A., Kapp, S. K., Orenski, K., & Laugeson, E. A. (2012). Social skills training for young adults with high-functioning autism spectrum disorders: A randomized controlled pilot study. *Journal of Autism and Developmental Disorders, 42*(6), 1094–1103. doi: 10.1007/s10803-011-1350-6

Ganz, J. B., Davis, J. L., Lund, E. M., Goodwyn, F. D., & Simpson, R. L. (2012). Meta-analysis of PECS with individuals with ASD: Investigation of targeted versus non-targeted outcomes, participant characteristics, and implementation phase. *Research in Developmental Disabilities, 33*(2), 406–418. doi: 10.1016/j.ridd.2011.09.023

Ganz, J. B., Earles-Vollrath, T. L., Heath, A. K., Parker, R. I., Rispoli, M. J., & Duran, J. B. (2012). A meta-analysis of single case research studies on aided augmentative and alternative communication systems with individuals with autism spectrum disorders. *Journal of Autism and Developmental Disorders, 42*(1), 60–74. doi: 10.1007/s10803-011-1212-2

Gargaro, B. A., Rinehart, N. J., Bradshaw, J. L., Tonge, B. J., & Sheppard, D. M. (2011). Autism and ADHD: How far have we come in the comorbidity debate? *Neuroscience Biobehavioral Reviews, 35*(5), 1081–1088. doi: 10.1016/j.neubiorev.2010.11.002

Gillberg, C., Billstedt, E., Sundh, V., & Gillberg, I. C. (2010). Mortality in autism: A prospective longitudinal community-based study. *Journal of Autism and Developmental Disorders, 40*(3), 352–357. doi: 10.1007/s10803-009-0883-4

Gilliam, J. E. (1995). *Gilliam Autism Rating Scale: Examiner's manual.* Los Angeles, CA: Pro-Ed.

Goldman, S. E., Richdale, A. L., Clemons, T., & Malow, B. A. (2012). Parental sleep concerns in autism spectrum disorders: Variations from childhood to adolescence. *Journal of Autism and Developmental Disorders, 42*(4), 531–538. doi: 10.1007/s10803-011-1270-5

Goldstein, H. (2002). Communication Intervention for children with autism: A review of treatment efficacy. *Journal of Autism and Developmental Disorders, 32*(5), 373–396. doi: 10.1023/A:1020589821992

Gotham, K., Pickles, A., & Lord, C. (2012). Trajectories of autism severity in children using standardized ADOS scores. *Pediatrics, 130*(5), e1278–e1284. doi: 10.1542/peds.2011-3668

Gray, C. (1998). Social stories and comic strip conversations with students with Asperger syndrome and high-functioning autism. In E. Schopler, G. Mesibov, & L. Kunce (Eds.), *Asperger syndrome or high-functioning autism?* (pp. 167–198). New York, NY: Plenum Press. doi: 10.1007/978-1-4615-5369-4_9

Green, V. A., Pituch, K. A., Itchon, J., Choi, A., O'Reilly, M., & Sigafoos, J. (2006). Internet survey of treatments used by parents of children with autism. *Research in Developmental Disabilities, 27*(1), 70–84. doi: 10.1016/j.ridd.2004.12.002

Grinker, R. R. (2007). *Unstrange minds: Remapping the world of autism.* New York, NY: Basic Press.

Grinker, R. R., Yeargin-Allsopp, M., & Boyle, C. (2011). Culture and autism spectrum disorders: The impact on prevalence and recognition. In D. Amaral, G. Dawson, & D. Geschwind (Eds.), *Autism spectrum disorders* (pp. 112–136). Oxford, UK: Oxford University Press. doi: 10.1093/med/9780195371826.003.0008

Grzadzinski, R., Di Martino, A., Brady, E., Mairena, M. A., O'Neale, M., Petkova, E., ... Castellanos, F. X. (2011). Examining autistic traits in children with ADHD: Does the autism spectrum extend to ADHD? *Journal of Autism and Developmental Disorders, 41*(9), 1178–1191. doi: 10.1007/s10803-010-1135-3

Gutstein, S. E. (2001). *Autism Aspergers: Solving the relationship puzzle: A new developmental program that opens the door to lifelong social and emotional growth.* Arlington, VA: Future Horizons.

Gutstein, S. E., Burgess, A. F., & Montfort, K. (2007). Evaluation of the relationship development intervention program. *Autism, 11*(5), 397–411. doi: 10.1177/1362361307079603

Hadjikhani, N., Joseph, R. M., Snyder, J., & Tager-Flusberg, H. (2006). Anatomical differences in the mirror neuron system and social cognition network in autism. *Cerebral Cortex, 16*(9), 1276–1282. doi: 10.1093/cercor/bhj069

Hall, S. E., & Riccio, C. A. (2012). Complementary and alternative treatment use for autism spectrum disorders. *Complementary Therapies in Clinical Practice, 18*(3), 159–163. doi: 10.1016/j.ctcp.2012.03.004

Hanson, E., Kalish, L. A., Bunce, E., Curtis, C., McDaniel, S., Ware, J., & Petry, J. (2007). Use of complementary and alternative medicine among children diagnosed with autism spectrum disorder. *Journal of Autism and Developmental Disorders, 37*(4), 628–636. doi: 10.1007/s10803-006-0192-0

Happe, F., & Frith, U. (2006). The weak coherence account: Detail-focused cognitive style in autism spectrum disorders. *Journal of Autism and Developmental Disorders, 36*(1), 5–25. doi: 10.1007/s10803-005-0039-0

Hendren, R. L. (2013). Autism: Biomedical complementary treatment approaches. *Child and Adolescent Psychiatric Clinics of North America, 22*(3), 443–456. doi: 10.1016/j.chc.2013.03.002

Howlin, P., Goode, S., Hutton, J., & Rutter, M. (2004). Adult outcome for children with autism. *Journal of Child Psychology and Psychiatry, 45*(2), 212–229. doi: 10.1111/j.1469-7610.2004.00215.x

Howlin, P., Gordon, R. K., Pasco, G., Wade, A., & Charman, T. (2007). The effectiveness of Picture Exchange Communication System (PECS) training for teachers of children with autism: A pragmatic, group randomised controlled trial. *Journal of Child Psychology and Psychiatry, 48*(5), 473–481. doi: 10.1111/j.1469-7610.2006.01707.x

Howlin, P., Magiati, I., & Charman, T. (2009). Systematic review of early intensive behavioral interventions for children with autism. *American Journal on Intellectual and Developmental Disabilities, 114*(1), 23–41. doi: 10.1352/2009.114:23-41

Hus, V., Bishop, S., Gotham, K., Huerta, M., & Lord, C. (2013). Factors influencing scores on the social responsiveness scale. *Journal of Child Psychology and Psychiatry, 54*(2), 216–224. doi: 10.1111/j.1469-7610.2012.02589.x

Individuals With Disabilities Education Act, 20 U.S.C. § 1400 (2004).

Ingersoll, B., & Schreibman, L. (2006). Teaching reciprocal imitation skills to young children with autism using a naturalistic behavioral approach: Effects on language, pretend play, and joint attention. *Journal of Autism and Developmental Disorders, 36*(4), 487–505. doi: 10.1007/s10803-006-0089-y

Interagency Autism Coordinating Committee. (2012). *IACC Strategic Plan for Autism Spectrum Disorder (ASD) Research: 2012 Update.* Retrieved from http://iacc.hhs.gov/strategic-plan/2012/index.shtml

Kanner, L., & Eisenberg, L. (1955). Review of psychiatric progress 1954: Child psychiatry and mental deficiency. *American Journal of Psychiatry, 111*(7), 520–523.

Kasari, C., Paparella, T., Freeman, S., & Jahromi, L. B. (2008). Language outcome in autism: Randomized comparison of joint attention and play interventions. *Journal of Consulting and Clinical Psychology, 76*(1), 125–137. doi: 10.1037/0022-006X.76.1.125

Kasari, C., & Patterson, S. (2012). Interventions addressing social impairment in autism. *Current Psychiatry Reports, 14*(6), 713–725. doi: 10.1007/s11920-012-0317-4

Kawamura, Y., Takahashi, O., & Ishii, T. (2008). Reevaluating the incidence of pervasive developmental disorders: Impact of elevated rates of detection through implementation of an integrated system of screening in Toyota, Japan. *Psychiatry and Clinical Neuroscience, 62*(2), 152–159. doi: 10.1111/j.1440-1819.2008.01748.x

Kelley, E., Paul, J. J., Fein, D., & Naigles, L. R. (2006). Residual language deficits in optimal outcome children with a history of autism. *Journal of Autism and Developmental Disorders, 36*(6), 807–828. doi: 10.1007/s10803-006-0111-4

Kim, J., Wigram, T., & Gold, C. (2009). Emotional, motivational and interpersonal responsiveness of children with autism in improvisational music therapy. *Autism, 13*(4), 389–409. doi: 10.1177/1362361309105660

Kim, S. H., & Lord, C. (2012). New autism diagnostic interview-revised algorithms for toddlers and young preschoolers from 12 to 47 months of age. *Journal of Autism and Developmental Disorders, 42*(1), 82–93. doi: 10.1007/s10803-011-1213-1

Kim, Y. S., Leventhal, B. L., Koh, Y. J., Fombonne, E., Laska, E., Lim, E. C., … Grinker, R. R. (2011). Prevalence of autism spectrum disorders in a total population sample. *American Journal of Psychiatry, 168*(9), 904–912.

Klinger, L. G., & Dawson, G. (1992). Facilitating early social and communicative development in children with autism. In S. F. Warren & J. E. Reichle (Eds.), *Causes and effects in communication and language intervention* (pp. 157–186). Baltimore, MD: Paul H. Brookes.

Koegel, R. L., & Koegel, L. K. (2006). *Pivotal response treatments for autism: Communication, social, & academic development.* Baltimore, MD: Paul H Brookes Publishing.

Koegel, L. K., Singh, A. K., & Koegel, R. L. (2010). Improving motivation for academics in children with autism. *Journal of Autism and Developmental Disorders, 40*(9), 1057–1066. doi: 10.1007/s10803-010-0962-6

Koegel, R. L., O'Dell, M. C., & Koegel, L. K. (1987). A natural language teaching paradigm for nonverbal autistic children. *Journal of Autism and Developmental Disorders, 17*(2), 187–200. doi: 10.1007/BF01495055

Kokina, A., & Kern, L. (2010). Social Story™ interventions for students with autism spectrum disorders: A meta-analysis. *Journal of Autism and Developmental Disorders, 40*(7), 812–826. doi: 10.1007/s10803-009-0931-0

Laugeson, E. A., Frankel, F., Gantman, A., Dillon, A. R., & Mogil, C. (2012). Evidence-based social skills training for adolescents with autism spectrum disorders: The UCLA PEERS program. *Journal of Autism and Developmental Disorders, 42*(6), 1025–1036. doi: 10.1007/s10803-011-1339-1

Leaf, R. B., & McEachin, J. (1999). *A work in progress: Behavior management strategies and a curriculum for intensive behavioral treatment of autism.* New York, NY: Drl Books.

Lerner, M. D., White, S. W., & McPartland, J. C. (2012). Mechanisms of change in psychosocial interventions for autism spectrum disorders. *Dialogues in Clinical Neuroscience, 14*(3), 307–318.

Levy, S. E., Giarelli, E., Lee, L. C., Schieve, L. A., Kirby, R. S., Cunniff, C., … Rice, C. E. (2010). Autism spectrum disorder and co-occurring developmental, psychiatric, and medical conditions among children in multiple populations of the United States. *Journal of Developmental and Behavioral Pediatrics, 31*(4), 267–275. doi: 10.1097/DBP.0b013e3181d5d03b

Levy, S. E., Mandell, D. S., Merhar, S., Ittenbach, R. F., & Pinto-Martin, J. A. (2003). Use of complementary and alternative medicine among children recently diagnosed with autistic spectrum disorder. *Journal of Developmental and Behavioral Pediatrics, 24*(6), 418–423. doi: 10.1097/00004703-200312000-00003

Lewin, A. B., Wood, J. J., Gunderson, S., Murphy, T. K., & Storch, E. A. (2011). Phenomenology of comorbid autism spectrum and obsessive-compulsive disorders among children. *Journal of Developmental and Physical Disabilities, 23*, 543–553. doi: 10.1007/s10882-011-9247-z

Leyfer, O. T., Tager-Flusberg, H., Dowd, M., Tomblin, J. B., & Folstein, S. E. (2008). Overlap between autism and specific language impairment: Comparison of Autism Diagnostic Interview and Autism Diagnostic Observation Schedule scores. *Autism Research, 1*(5), 284–296. doi: 10.1002/aur.43

Lord, C. (1995). Follow-up of two-year-olds referred for possible autism. *Journal of Child Psychology and Psychiatry, 36*(8), 1365–1382. doi: 10.1111/j.1469-7610.1995.tb01669.x

Lord, C., & Jones, R. M. (2012). Annual Research Review: Re-thinking the classification of autism spectrum disorders. *Journal of Child Psychology and Psychiatry, 53*(5), 490–509. doi: 10.1111/j.1469-7610.2012.02547.x

Lord, C., Luyster, R., Guthrie, W., & Pickles, A. (2012). Patterns of developmental trajectories in toddlers with autism spectrum disorder. *Journal of Consulting and Clinical Psychology, 80*(3), 477–489. doi: 10.1037/a0027214

Lord, C., Petkova, E., Hus, V., Gan, W., Lu, F., Martin, D. M., … Risi, S. (2012). A multisite study of the clinical diagnosis of different autism spectrum disorders. *Archives of General Psychiatry, 69*(3), 306–313. doi: 10.1001/archgenpsychiatry.2011.148

Lord, C., Risi, S., DiLavore, P., Shulman, C., Thurm, A., & Pickles, A. (2006). Autism from 2 to 9 years of age. *Archives of General Psychiatry, 63*(6), 694. doi: 10.1001/archpsyc.63.6.694

Lord, C., Risi, S., Lambrecht, L., Cook, E. H., Jr., Leventhal, B. L., DiLavore, P. C., … Rutter, M. (2000). The autism diagnostic observation schedule generic: A standard measure of social and communication deficits associated with the spectrum of autism. *Journal of Autism and Developmental Disorders, 30*, 205–223. doi: 10.1023/A:1005592401947

Lord, C., Rutter, M., DiLavore, P. C., Risi, S., Gotham, K., & Bishop, S. L. (2012). *Autism Diagnostic Observation Schedule, second edition (ADOS-2) manual (Part 1): Modules 1–4*. Torrance, CA: Western Psychological Services.

Lovaas, O. I. (1987). Behavioral treatment and normal educational and intellectual functioning in young autistic children. *Journal of Consulting and Clinical Psychology, 55*(1), 3–9. doi: 10.1037/0022-006X.55.1.3

Mahajan, R., Bernal, M. P., Panzer, R., Whitaker, A., Roberts, W., Handen, B., … Veenstra-Vanderweele, J. (2012). Clinical practice pathways for evaluation and medication choice for attention-deficit/hyperactivity disorder symptoms in autism spectrum disorders. *Pediatrics, 130*(Suppl 2), S125–S138. doi: 10.1542/peds.2012-0900J

Malow, B., Adkins, K., McGrew, S., Wang, L., Goldman, S., Fawkes, D., & Burnette, C. (2012). Melatonin for sleep in children with autism: A controlled trial examining dose, tolerability, and outcomes. *Journal of Autism and Developmental Disorders, 42*(8), 1729–1737. doi: 10.1007/s10803-011-1418-3

Mandell, D. S., Listerud, J., Levy, S. E., & Pinto-Martin, J. A. (2002). Race differences in the age at diagnosis among medicaid-eligible children with autism. *Journal of the American Academy of Child and Adolescent Psychiatry, 41*(12), 1447–1453. doi: 10.1097/00004583-200212000-00016

Mandell, D. S., Wiggins, L. D., Carpenter, L. A., Daniels, J., DiGuiseppi, C., Durkin, M. S., … Kirby, R. S. (2009). Racial/ethnic disparities in the identification of children with autism spectrum disorders. *American Journal of Public Health, 99*(3), 493–498. doi: 10.2105/AJPH.2007.131243

Marcus, R. N., Owen, R., Kamen, L., Manos, G., McQuade, R. D., Carson, W. H., & Aman, M. G. (2009). A placebo-controlled, fixed-dose study of aripiprazole in children and adolescents with irritability associated with autistic disorder. *Journal of the American Academy of Child and Adolescent Psychiatry, 48*(11), 1110–1119. doi: 10.1097/CHI.0b013e3181b76658

Maurice, C., Green, G., & Luce, S. (1996). *Behavioral intervention for young children with autism*. Austin, TX: PRO-ED, Inc.

Martin, I., & McDonald, S. (2004). An exploration of causes of non-literal language problems in individuals with Asperger Syndrome. *Journal of Autism and Developmental Disorders, 34*(3), 311–328. doi: 10.1023/B:JADD.0000029553.52889.15

Mayo, J., Chlebowski, C., Fein, D. A., & Eigsti, I. M. (2013). Age of first words predicts cognitive ability and adaptive skills in children with ASD. *Journal of Autism and Developmental Disorders, 43*(2), 253–264. doi: 10.1007/s10803-012-1558-0

McCracken, J. T., McGough, J., Shah, B., Cronin, P., Hong, D., Aman, M. G., … McMahon, D. (2002). Risperidone in children with autism and serious behavioral problems. *New England Journal of Medicine, 347*(5), 314–321. doi: 10.1056/NEJMoa013171

McDougle, C. J., Brodkin, E. S., Naylor, S. T., Carlson, D. C., Cohen, D. J., & Price, L. H. (1998). Sertraline in adults with pervasive developmental disorders: A prospective open-label investigation. *Journal of Clinical Psychopharmacology, 18*(1), 62–66. doi: 10.1097/00004714-199802000-00010

McGovern, C. W., & Sigman, M. (2005). Continuity and change from early childhood to adolescence in autism. *Journal of Child Psychology and Psychiatry, 46*(4), 401–408. doi: 10.1111/j.1469-7610.2004.00361.x

Medeiros, K., Kozlowski, A. M., Beighley, J. S., Rojahn, J., & Matson, J. L. (2012). The effects of developmental quotient and diagnostic criteria on challenging behaviors in toddlers with developmental disabilities. *Research in Developmental Disabilities, 33*(4), 1110–1116. doi: 10.1016/j.ridd.2012.02.005

Mendelsohn, N. J., & Schaefer, G. B. (2008). Genetic evaluation of autism. *Seminars in Pediatric Neurology, 15*(1), 27–31. doi: 10.1016/j.spen.2008.01.005

Mesibov, G. B., & Shea, V. (2010). The TEACCH program in the era of evidence-based practice. *Journal of Autism and Developmental Disorders, 40*(5), 570–579. doi: 10.1007/s10803-009-0901-6

Minshew, N. J., & Keller, T. A. (2010). The nature of brain dysfunction in autism: Functional brain imaging studies. *Current Opinions in Neurology, 23*(2), 124–130. doi: 10.1097/WCO.0b013e32833782d4

Mitchell, S., Cardy, J. O., & Zwaigenbaum, L. (2011). Differentiating autism spectrum disorder from other developmental delays in the first two years of life. *Developmental Disability Research Review, 17*(2), 130–140. doi: 10.1002/ddrr.1107

MMWR. (2012). Prevalence of autism spectrum disorders: Autism and Developmental Disabilities Monitoring Network, 14 sites, United States, 2008. *MMWR Surveillance Summary, 61*(3), 1–19.

Montes, G., & Halterman, J. S. (2007). Psychological functioning and coping among mothers of children with autism: A population-based study. *Pediatrics, 119*(5), e1040–e1046. doi: 10.1542/peds.2006-2819

Mudford, O. C., Cross, B. A., Breen, S., Cullen, C., Reeves, D., Gould, J., & Douglas, J. (2000). Auditory integration training for children with autism: No behavioral benefits detected. *American Journal on Mental Retardation, 105*(2), 118–129. doi: 10.1352/0895-8017(2000)105<0118:AITFCW>2.0.CO;2

Mulloy, A., Lang, R., O'Reilly, M., Sigafoos, J., Lancioni, G., & Rispoli, M. (2010). Gluten-free and casein-free diets in the treatment of autism spectrum disorders: A systematic review. *Research in Autism Spectrum Disorders, 4*(3), 328–339. doi: 10.1016/j.rasd.2009.10.008

Munson, J., Dawson, G., Sterling, L., Beauchaine, T., Zhou, A., Koehler, E., … Frances, C. (2008). Evidence for latent classes of IQ in young children with autism spectrum disorder. *American Journal on Mental Retardation, 113*(6), 439–452. doi: 10.1352/2008.113:439-452

Murch, S. H., Anthony, A., Casson, D. H., Malik, M., Berelowitz, M., Dhillon, A. P., … Walker-Smith, J. A. (2004). Retraction of an interpretation. *Lancet, 363*, 750. doi: 10.1016/S0140-6736(04)15715-2

National Research Council. (2001). *Educating children with autism: Committee on educational interventions for children with autism.* Washington, DC: National Academy Press.

Nickels, K., Katusic, S. K., Colligan, R. C., Weaver, A. L., Voigt, R. G., & Barbaresi, W. J. (2008). Stimulant medication treatment of target behaviors in children with autism: A population-based study. *Journal of Developmental and Behavioral Pediatrics, 29*(2), 75–81. doi: 10.1097/DBP.0b013e31815f24f7

Odom, S. L., Boyd, B. A., Hall, L. J., & Hume, K. (2010). Evaluation of comprehensive treatment models for individuals with autism spectrum disorders. *Journal of Autism and Developmental Disorders, 40*(4), 425–436. doi: 10.1007/s10803-009-0825-1

Office of Autism Research Coordination (OARC), National Institute of Mental Health and Thomson Reuters, Inc. on behalf of the Interagency Autism Coordinating Committee (IACC). (2012). *IACC/OARC autism spectrum disorder research publications analysis report: The global landscape of autism research.* Retrieved from http://iacc.hhs.gov/publications-analysis/july2012/index.shtml

Ospina, M. B., Krebs Seida, J., Clark, B., Karkhaneh, M., Hartling, L., Tjosvold, L., … Smith, V. (2008). Behavioural and developmental interventions for autism spectrum disorder: A clinical systematic review. *PLoS ONE, 3*(11), e3755. doi: 10.1371/journal.pone.0003755

Osterling, J. A., Dawson, G., & Munson, J. A. (2002). Early recognition of 1-year-old infants with autism spectrum disorder versus mental retardation. *Developmental Psychopathology, 14*(2), 239–251. doi: 10.1017/S0954579402002031

Ozonoff, S., Goodlin-Jones, B. L., & Solomon, M. (2005). Evidence-based assessment of autism spectrum disorders in children and adolescents. *Journal of Clinical Child and Adolescent Psychology, 34*(3), 523–540. doi: 10.1207/s15374424jccp3403_8

Pajareya, K., & Nopmaneejumruslers, K. (2011). A pilot randomized controlled trial of DIR/Floortime parent training intervention for pre-school children with autistic spectrum disorders. *Autism, 15*(5), 563–577. doi: 10.1177/1362361310386502

Pajareya, K., & Nopmaneejumruslers, K. (2012). A one-year prospective follow-up study of a DIR/Floortime parent training intervention for pre-school children with autistic spectrum disorders. *Journal of the Medical Association of Thailand, 95*(9), 1184–1193.

Pampiglione, G., & Moynahan, E. J. (1976). The tuberous sclerosis syndrome: Clinical and EEG studies in 100 children. *Journal of Neurology Neurosurgery and Psychiatry, 39*(7), 666–673. doi: 10.1136/jnnp.39.7.666

Pardo, C. A. (2007). The neurobiology of autism. *Brain pathology, 17*(4), 434. doi: 10.1111/j.1750-3639.2007.00102.x

Pardo, C. A., Vargas, D. L., & Zimmerman, A. W. (2005). Immunity, neuroglia and neuro-inflammation in autism. *International Review of Psychiatry, 17*(6), 485–495. doi: 10.1080/02646830500381930

Parmeggiani, A., Barcia, G., Posar, A., Raimondi, E., Santucci, M., & Scaduto, M. C. (2010). Epilepsy and EEG paroxysmal abnormalities in autism spectrum disorders. *Brain Development, 32*(9), 783–789. doi: 10.1016/j.braindev.2010.07.003

Patterson, S. Y., Smith, V., & Jelen, M. (2010). Behavioural intervention practices for ste-reotypic and repetitive behaviour in individuals with autism spectrum disorder: A sys-tematic review. *Developmental Medicine and Child Neurology, 52*(4), 318–327. doi: 10.1111/j.1469-8749.2009.03597.x

Pelphrey, K., Sasson, N., Reznick, J. S., Paul, G., Goldman, B., & Piven, J. (2002). Visual scanning of faces in autism. *Journal of Autism and Developmental Disorders, 32*(4), 249–261. doi: 10.1023/A:1016374617369

Politte, L. C., & McDougle, C. J. (2013). Atypical antipsychotics in the treatment of chil-dren and adolescents with pervasive developmental disorders. *Psychopharmacology.* Advance online publication. doi: 10.1007/s00213-013-3068-y

Posey, D., Aman, M., McCracken, J., Scahill, L., Tierney, E., Arnold, L. E., … McDougle, C. (2007). Positive effects of methylphenidate on inattention and hyperactivity in per-vasive developmental disorders: An analysis of secondary measures. *Biological Psychiatry, 61*(4), 538–544. doi: 10.1016/j.biopsych.2006.09.028

Prizant, B. M., Wetherby, A. M., Rubin, E., & Laurent, A. C. (2003). The SCERTS Model: A transactional, family-centered approach to enhancing communication and socioemo-tional abilities of children with autism spectrum disorder. *Infants and Young Children, 16*(4), 296–316. doi: 10.1097/00001163-200310000-00004

Quirmbach, L. M., Lincoln, A. J., Feinberg-Gizzo, M. J., Ingersoll, B. R., & Andrews, S. M. (2009). Social stories: Mechanisms of effectiveness in increasing game play skills in children diagnosed with autism spectrum disorder using a pretest posttest repeated meas-ures randomized control group design. *Journal of Autism and Developmental Disorders, 39*(2), 299–321. doi: 10.1007/s10803-008-0628-9

Regier, D. A., Narrow, W. E., Clarke, D. E., Kraemer, H. C., Kuramoto, S. J., Kuhl, E. A., & Kupfer, D. J. (2013). DSM-5 field trials in the United States and Canada. Part II: Test-retest reliability of selected categorical diagnoses. *American Journal of Psychiatry, 170*(1), 59–70. doi: 10.1176/appi.ajp.2012.12070999

Reichow, B., Barton, E. E., Boyd, B. A., & Hume, K. (2012). Early intensive behavioral in-tervention (EIBI) for young children with autism spectrum disorders (ASD). *Cochrane Database of Systematic Reviews, 10*, CD009260. doi: 10.1002/14651858.CD009260. pub2

Reichow, B., Steiner, A. M., & Volkmar, F. (2012). Social skills groups for people aged 6 to 21 with autism spectrum disorders (ASD). *Cochrane Database of Systematic Reviews, 7*, CD008511. doi: 10.1002/14651858.CD008511.pub2

Reisinger, L. M., Cornish, K. M., & Fombonne, E. (2011). Diagnostic differentiation of au-tism spectrum disorders and pragmatic language impairment. *Journal of Autism and Developmental Disorders, 41*(12), 1694–1704. doi: 10.1007/s10803-011-1196-y

Research Units on Pediatric Psychopharmacology Autism Network. (2005). Randomized, controlled, crossover trial of methylphenidate in pervasive developmental disorders with hyperactivity. *Archives in General Psychiatry, 62*(11), 1266–1274.

Richler, J., Huerta, M., Bishop, S. L., & Lord, C. (2010). Developmental trajectories of re-stricted and repetitive behaviors and interests in children with autism spectrum disor-ders. *Development and Psychopathology, 22*(01), 55–69. doi: 10.1017/S0954579409990265

Risi, S., Lord, C., Gotham, K., Corsello, C., Chrysler, C., Szatmari, P., … Pickles, A. (2006). Combining information from multiple sources in the diagnosis of autism spectrum dis-orders. *Journal of the American Academy of Child and Adolescent Psychiatry, 45*(9), 1094–1103. doi: 10.1097/01.chi.0000227880.42780.0e

Robins, D., Fein, D., Barton, M., & Green, J. (2001). The Modified Checklist for Autism in Toddlers: An initial study investigating the early detection of autism and pervasive developmental disorders. *Journal of Autism and Developmental Disorders, 31*(2), 131–144. doi: 10.1023/A:1010738829569

Robinson, E. B., Lichtenstein, P., Anckarsater, H., Happe, F., & Ronald, A. (2013). Examining and interpreting the female protective effect against autistic behavior. *Proceedings of the National Academy of Sciences, 110*(13), 5258–5262. doi: 10.1073/pnas.1211070110

Rogers, S. J., Estes, A., Lord, C., Vismara, L., Winter, J., Fitzpatrick, A., ... Dawson, G. (2012). Effects of a brief early start Denver model (ESDM)-based parent intervention on toddlers at risk for autism spectrum disorders: A randomized controlled trial. *Journal of the American Academy of Child and Adolescent Psychiatry, 51*(10), 1052–1065. doi: 10.1016/j.jaac.2012.08.003

Rogers, S. J., Hayden, D., Hepburn, S., Charlifue-Smith, R., Hall, T., & Hayes, A. (2006). Teaching young nonverbal children with autism useful speech: A pilot study of the Denver model and PROMPT interventions. *Journal of Autism and Developmental Disorders, 36*(8), 1007–1024. doi: 10.1007/s10803-006-0142-x

Romanczyk, R.G., Arnstein, L.M., Valluripalli, L., & Gillis, J. (2003). The myriad of controversial treatments for autism: A critical evaluation of efficacy. In S. O. Lillienfeld, S. J. Lohr, & J. M. Lynn (Eds.), *Science and pseudoscience in contemporary clinical psychology* (pp. 363–398). New York, NY: Guilford Press.

Rutter, M. (1968). Concepts of autism: A review of research. *Journal of Child Psychology and Psychiatry, 9*(1), 1–25. doi: 10.1111/j.1469-7610.1968.tb02204.x

Rutter, M. (2011). Autism spectrum disorders: Looking backward and looking forward. In D. G. Amaral, G. Dawson, & D. H. Geschwind (Eds.), *Autism spectrum disorders* (17–29). New York, NY: Oxford University Press.

Rutter, M., LeCouteur, A., & Lord, C. (2003a). *Autism Diagnostic Interview Revised WPS*. Los Angeles, CA: Western Psychological Services.

Rutter, M., LeCouteur, A., & Lord, C. (2003b). *Social Communication Questionnaire (SCQ)*. Los Angeles, CA.: Western Psychological Services.

Sautter, R. A., & Leblanc, L. A. (2006). Empirical applications of Skinner's analysis of verbal behavior with humans. *Analysis of Verbal Behavior, 22*, 35–48.

Schopler, E., Reichler, R., & Renner, B. (1988). *Childhood Autism Rating Scale (CARS)*. Los Angeles, CA: Pro-Ed.

Shao, L., Martin, M. V., Watson, S. J., Schatzberg, A., Akil, H., Myers, R. M., ... Vawter, M. P. (2008). Mitochondrial involvement in psychiatric disorders. *Annals of Medicine, 40*(4), 281–295. doi: 10.1080/07853890801923753

Shumway, S., Farmer, C., Thurm, A., Joseph, L., Black, D., & Golden, C. (2012). The ADOS calibrated severity score: Relationship to phenotypic variables and stability over time. *Autism Research, 5*(4), 267–276. doi: 10.1002/aur.1238

Siegel, M., & Beaulieu, A. A. (2012). Psychotropic medications in children with autism spectrum disorders: A systematic review and synthesis for evidence-based practice. *Journal of Autism and Developmental Disorders, 42*(8), 1592–1605. doi: 10.1007/s10803-011-1399-2

Sikora, D. M., Johnson, K., Clemons, T., & Katz, T. (2012). The relationship between sleep problems and daytime behavior in children of different ages with autism spectrum disorders. *Pediatrics, 130*(Suppl 2), S83–S90. doi: 10.1542/peds.2012-0900F

Smith, I. M., Koegel, R. L., Koegel, L. K., Openden, D. A., Fossum, K. L., & Bryson, S. E. (2010). Effectiveness of a novel community-based early intervention model for children with autistic spectrum disorder. *American Journal on Intellectual and Developmental Disabilities, 115*(6), 504–523. doi: 10.1352/1944-7558-115.6.504

Sofronoff, K., Leslie, A., & Brown, W. (2004). Parent management training and Asperger syndrome: A randomized controlled trial to evaluate a parent based intervention. *Autism, 8*(3), 301–317. doi: 10.1177/1362361304045215

Stahmer, A. C. (1995). Teaching symbolic play skills to children with autism using pivotal response training. *Journal of Autism and Developmental Disorders, 25*(2), 123–141. doi: 10.1007/BF02178500

Strain, P. S., & Bovey, E. H. (2011). Randomized, controlled trial of the leap model of early intervention for young children with autism spectrum disorders. *Topics in Early Childhood Special Education, 31*(3), 133–154. doi: 10.1177/0271121411408740

Sukhodolsky, D. G., Bloch, M. H., Panza, K. E., & Reichow, B. (2013). Cognitive-behavioral therapy for anxiety in children with high-functioning autism: A meta-analysis. *Pediatrics, 132*(5), e1341–e1350. doi: 10.1542/peds.2013-1193

Sun, X., Allison, C., Matthews, F. E., Sharp, S. J., Auyeung, B., Baron-Cohen, S., & Brayne, C. (2013). Prevalence of autism in mainland China, Hong Kong and Taiwan: A systematic review and meta-analysis. *Molecular Autism, 4*(1), 7. doi: 10.1186/2040-2392-4-7

Sundberg, M. L. (2008). *VB-MAPP Verbal Behavior Milestones Assessment and Placement Program: A language and social skills assessment program for children with autism or other developmental disabilities: Guide.* Concord, CA: AVB Press.

Thurm, A., Lord, C., Lee, L. C., & Newschaffer, C. (2007). Predictors of language acquisition in preschool children with autism spectrum disorders. *Journal of Autism and Developmental Disorders, 37*(9), 1721–1734. doi: 10.1007/s10803-006-0300-1

Tsiouris, J. A., Kim, S. Y., Brown, W. T., Pettinger, J., & Cohen, I. L. (2013). Prevalence of psychotropic drug use in adults with intellectual disability: Positive and negative findings from a large scale study. *Journal of Autism and Developmental Disorders, 43*(3), 719–731. doi: 10.1007/s10803-012-1634-5

Van Bourgondien, M. E., Reichle, N. C., & Schopler, E. (2003). Effects of a model treatment approach on adults with autism. *Journal of Autism and Developmental Disorders, 33*(2), 131–140. doi: 10.1023/A:1022931224934

Vargas, D. L., Nascimbene, C., Krishnan, C., Zimmerman, A. W., & Pardo, C. A. (2005). Neuroglial activation and neuroinflammation in the brain of patients with autism. *Annals of Neurology, 57*(1), 67–81. doi: 10.1002/ana.20315

Warren, Z., McPheeters, M. L., Sathe, N., Foss-Feig, J. H., Glasser, A., & Veenstra-Vanderweele, J. (2011). A systematic review of early intensive intervention for autism spectrum disorders. *Pediatrics, 127*(5), 1303–1311. doi: 10.1542/peds.2011-0426

Warren, Z., Veenstra-Vanderweele, J., Stone, W., Bruzek, J. L., Nahmias, A. S., Foss-Feig, J. H., … McPheeters, M. L. (2011). *AHRQ Comparative Effectiveness Reviews: Therapies for children with autism spectrum disorders.* Rockville, MD: Agency for Healthcare Research and Quality.

Wetherby, A. M., Allen, L., Cleary, J., Kublin, K., & Goldstein, H. (2002). Validity and reliability of the communication and symbolic behavior scales developmental profile with very young children. *Journal of Speech, Language and Hearing Research*, 45(6), 1202. doi: 10.1044/1092-4388(2002/097)

Wetherby, A. M., Brosnan-Maddox, S., Peace, V., & Newton, L. (2008). Validation of the Infant–Toddler Checklist as a broadband screener for autism spectrum disorders from 9 to 24 months of age. *Autism*, 12(5), 487–511. doi: 10.1177/1362361308094501

Wetherby, A. M., Woods, J., Allen, L., Cleary, J., Dickinson, H., & Lord, C. (2004). Early indicators of autism spectrum disorders in the second year of life. *Journal of Autism and Developmental Disorders, 34*(5), 473–493. doi: 10.1007/s10803-004-2544-y

White, S. W., Keonig, K., & Scahill, L. (2007). Social skills development in children with autism spectrum disorders: A review of the intervention research. *Journal of Autism and Developmental Disorders, 37*(10), 1858–1868. doi: 10.1007/s10803-006-0320-x

White, S. W., Oswald, D., Ollendick, T., & Scahill, L. (2009). Anxiety in children and adolescents with autism spectrum disorders. *Clinical Psychology Review, 29*(3), 216–229. doi: 10.1016/j.cpr.2009.01.003

Whitehouse, A. J. (2013). Complementary and alternative medicine for autism spectrum disorders: Rationale, safety and efficacy. *Journal of Paediatric Child Health, 49* (9), 438–442. doi: 10.1111/jpc.12242

Williams, K., Wray, J., & Wheeler, D. (2005). Intravenous secretin for autism spectrum disorder. *Cochrane Database of Systematic Reviews, 3*.

Wing, L., Leekam, S. R., Libby, S. J., Gould, J., & Larcombe, M. (2002). The Diagnostic Interview for Social and Communication Disorders: Background, inter-rater reliability and clinical use. *Journal of Child Psychology and Psychiatry, 43*(3), 307–325. doi: 10.1111/1469-7610.00023

Wood, J. J., Drahota, A., Sze, K., Har, K., Chiu, A., & Langer, D. A. (2009). Cognitive behavioral therapy for anxiety in children with autism spectrum disorders: A randomized, controlled trial. *Journal of Child Psychology and Psychiatry, 50*(3), 224–234. doi: 10.1111/j.1469-7610.2008.01948.x

WHO–World Health Organization. (1977). *Manual of the international statistical classification of diseases, and related health problems ninth revision (Vol. 1).* Geneva, Switzerland: Author.

WHO–World Health Organization. (1993). *Manual of the international statistical classification of diseases, and related health problems 10th revision (Vol. 1).* Geneva, Switzerland: Author.

WHO–World Health Organization. (2010). *ICD-10 classification of mental and behavioural disorders diagnostic criteria for research.* Geneva, Switzerland: Author.

Yoder, P. J., & Layton, T. L. (1988). Speech following sign language training in autistic children with minimal verbal language. *Journal of Autism and Developmental Disorders, 18*(2), 217–229. doi: 10.1007/BF02211948

Zandt, F., Prior, M., & Kyrios, M. (2007). Repetitive behaviour in children with high functioning autism and obsessive compulsive disorder. *Journal of Autism and Developmental Disorders, 37*(2), 251–259. doi: 10.1007/s10803-006-0158-2

Zwaigenbaum, L., Bryson, S. E., Szatmari, P., Brian, J., Smith, I. M., Roberts, W., ... Roncadin, C. (2012). Sex differences in children with autism spectrum disorder identified within a high-risk infant cohort. *Journal of Autism and Developmental Disorders, 42*(12), 2585–2596. doi: 10.1007/s10803-012-1515-y

7

Appendix: Tools and Resources

Appendix 1: Tools and Resources

Appendix 1

Tools and Resources

A Clinician's Guide to Providing Effective Feedback: Feedback Session Quality Checklist
This is a checklist for clinicians with guidelines for providing feedback to families of children newly diagnosed with an autism spectrum disorder (see pp. 14–16). The checklist divides the feedback session into four components: preparing for the feedback session, beginning the session, presenting the diagnosis, and discussing the next steps. Each component has a related checklist with several recommendations for the clinician.
http://www.autismspeaks.org/sites/default/files/docs/sciencedocs/atn/delivering_feedback_manual.pdf

Agency for Healthcare Research and Quality
This website provides a summary of the effectiveness of different interventions for children with ASD who are between 2 and 12 years of age.
http://effectivehealthcare.ahrq.gov/ehc/products/106/651/Autism_Disorder_exec-summ.pdf

American Academy of Pediatrics
This is the official website of the American Academy of Pediatrics. It provides information and resources for children with ASD.
http://www.aap.org

Autism Speaks
This is the official website of the Autism Speaks organization. The website provides overviews and links to some of the most recent news and research for individuals with ASD. Family services and resources are also offered on the website.
http://www.autismspeaks.org

Autism Speaks™ 100 Day Kit: Unique Abilities That May Accompany Autism
This chart provides a list of some of the strengths and abilities that children with autism spectrum disorder may have (see p. 9).
http://www.autismspeaks.org/sites/default/files/100_day_kit_section_1.pdf

Centers for Disease Control and Prevention
This website provides information and data regarding the epidemiology, causes, and known risk factors of ASD.
http://www.cdc.gov/ncbddd/autism/research.html

Early Warning Signs of Autism Spectrum Disorder: Handout I – First Signs Hallmark Developmental Milestones
This handout from the Centers for Disease Control and Prevention provides an overview of several social and communication developmental milestones for children between 4 and 36 months of age (see pp. 18–19).

http://www.cdc.gov/ncbddd/actearly/act/documents/handouts/ews_hand-outs_508_final.pdf

FIRST WORDS Project

The FIRST WORDS Project at Florida State University is a longitudinal study whose goal it is to identify early warning signs of ASD and language disorders. The website provides information and research on communication delays as well as resources for parents.
http://firstwords.fsu.edu/

Interagency Autism Coordinating Committee

This is the official website of the Interagency Autism Coordinating Committee, the federal advisory committee for ASD.
http://iacc.hhs.gov

Modified Checklist for Autism in Toddlers, Revised With Follow-Up (M-CHAT-R/F)

This checklist is a parent report screening measure that can be used for children between 16 and 30 months of age. The measure consists of 20 questions covering social communication development, the presence of restricted and repetitive behaviors, and motor development.
https://www.m-chat.org/_references/mchatdotorg.pdf

National Professional Development Center on Autism Spectrum Disorders

The NPDC on Autism Spectrum Disorders provides and develops resources for practitioners and services providers based on evidence-based practice. The resources are meant to be used with children and adolescents with ASD.
http://autismpdc.fpg.unc.edu

National Standards Report

This report reviews and analyzes research on treating and evaluating children and adults with ASD.
http://www.nationalautismcenter.org/nsp/

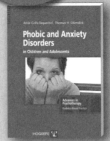

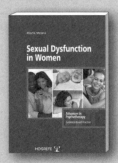
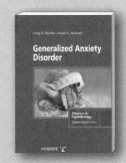
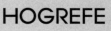

View all volumes at www.hogrefe.com/series/apt

Hogrefe Publishing
30 Amberwood Parkway · Ashland, OH 44805 · USA
Tel: (800) 228-3749 · Fax: (419) 281-6883
E-Mail: customerservice@hogrefe.com

Hogrefe Publishing
Merkelstr. 3 · 37085 Göttingen · Germany
Tel: +49 551 999 500 · Fax: +49 551 999 50 111
E-Mail: customerservice@hogrefe.de

Hogrefe Publishing c/o Marston Book Services Ltd
160 Eastern Ave., Milton Park· Abingdon, OX14 4SB · UK
Tel: +44 1235 465577 · Fax +44 1235 465556
direct.orders@marston.co.uk

Order online at **www.hogrefe.com**
or call toll-free **(800) 228-3749** (US only)

Sven Bölte & Joachim Hallmayer (Editors)

Autism Spectrum Conditions

FAQs on Autism, Asperger Syndrome, and Atypical Autism Answered by International Experts

2011, x + 283 pages, ISBN 978-0-88937-393-8
US $49.00 / £ 27.90 / € 34.95

For all who work with autism spectrum clients – 78 FAQs about autism, Asperger, and pervasive developmental disorder answered by 66 of the world's leading experts!

Autism Spectrum Conditions (ASC), which include autism, Asperger syndrome, and pervasive developmental disorder, are puzzling, controversial, and a challenge – and the subject of both increasing interest and a multitude of myths. While many questions about ASC remain unanswered to date, our knowledge of the roots, characteristics, outcome, and effective intervention options has improved hugely in recent years.

In this unique book, leading clinical and research authorities help explode myths and answer frequently asked questions on ASC: What are ASC? What are their causes? How prevalent are they? How are ASC diagnosed and by whom? What are the first signs? How should people with ASC be educated and treated? How do people with ASC think? What can parents, teachers, and experts do? What can be done for adults with ASC? Where can information and support be found?

These and other areas are covered by this clearly written book to provide concise, scientifically sound, state-of-the-art, and practical information about autism spectrum conditions for all who work with ASC clients, as well as for families and friends.

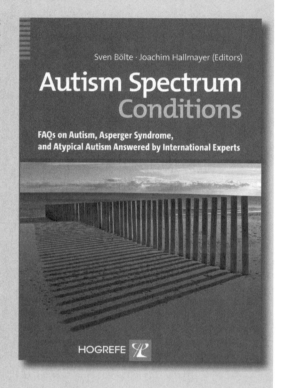

Table of Contents

Hogrefe Publishing
30 Amberwood Parkway · Ashland, OH 44805 · USA
Tel: (800) 228-3749 · Fax: (419) 281-6883
E-Mail: customerservice@hogrefe.com

Hogrefe Publishing
Merkelstr.3 · 37085 Göttingen · Germany
Tel: +49 551 999 500 · Fax: +49 551 999 50 111
E-Mail: customerservice@hogrefe.de

Hogrefe Publishing c/o Marston Book Services Ltd
160 Eastern Ave., Milton Park · Abingdon, OX14 4SB · UK
Tel: +44 1235 465577 · Fax +44 1235 465556
E-mail: direct.orders@marston.co.uk

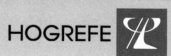

Order online at **www.hogrefe.com**
or call toll-free **(800) 228-3749** (US only)